Bitter Money

Cultural Economy and Some African Meanings of Forbidden Commodities

Parker Shipton

American Ethnological Society Monograph Series, Number 1
James L. Watson, Series Editor

Library of Congress Cataloging-in-Publication Data
Shipton, Parker MacDonald.
  Bitter money : cultural economy and some African meanings of forbidden
commodities / Parker Shipton.
    p.   cm.—(American Ethnological Society monograph series ; no. 1)
  Bibliography: p.
  ISBN 0-913167-29-0
  1. Luo (African people)—Money. 2. Luo (African people)—Economic con-
ditions. 3. Economic anthropology—Kenya. 4. Kenya—Economic conditions.
I. Title. II. Series.
DT433.545.L85S53   1989
306.3—dc20   89-6680

Copies may be ordered from:

American Anthropological Association
1703 New Hampshire Avenue, N.W.
Washington, D.C. 20009

Contents

Acknowledgments

The funding that made this study possible was provided by the Marshall Aid Commemoration Commission of the United Kingdom, St. John's College of Cambridge University and its Warmington Research Studentship, the Wenner-Gren Foundation for Anthropological Research, the Smuts Memorial Fund of Cambridge University, and the Radcliffe-Brown Memorial Fund of the Royal Anthropological Institute. The Kenyan field research was conducted while I held a Research Associateship at the Institute of African Studies, University of Nairobi, between 1980 and 1983.

Special thanks are due to Polly Steele, my wife, fieldwork companion, and mercilessly discerning editorial critic; to Emin Ochieng, who first helped me perceive beliefs about bitter money and collaborated closely on this topic in the Luo country; and to Janes Athiambo, Joseph Obura, Jeremiah and Jedidah Okumu, Elly Owino, and my other hosts and friends in western Kenya. In the Gambia, Fally Khan, Momodou Sanyang, and Bakari Sidibe offered keen insights and contacts as well as hospitality.

For useful comments and suggestions, I thank many, including Ray Abrahams, Patrick Alila, John Beattie, John Bowen, Abena Busia, Naa-Morkor Busia, Jack Glazier, Stephen Gudeman, Margaret Jean Hay, Caroline Humphrey, Shem Migot-Adholla, G. E. M. Ogutu, H. W. O. Okoth-Ogendo, David Parkin, A. F. Robertson, Malcolm Ruel, Lamin Sanneh, Nancy Schwartz, James Shipton, Tal Tamari, David Throup, and Richard Waller. The series editor, James Watson, and the anonymous referees provided helpful advice for revision. I am grateful to my colleagues at the Harvard Institute for International Development and the Department of Anthropology, Harvard University, for their ideas and support. Of these, Sally Falk Moore and Pauline Peters added useful information from their fieldwork; and Edmund Carlevale, Anne Lewinson, Bradley Nixon, John Pollard, and Suzanne Sloan gave much appreciated help at different times.

Parts of this work have been presented at the American Anthropological Association annual meeting, and seminars at the African Studies Centers at Boston University and Cambridge University, and the Departments of Anthropology at Yale University and the University of North Carolina at Chapel Hill. At each instance I received constructive comments.

None of these people or institutions is responsible for any errors or opinions expressed.

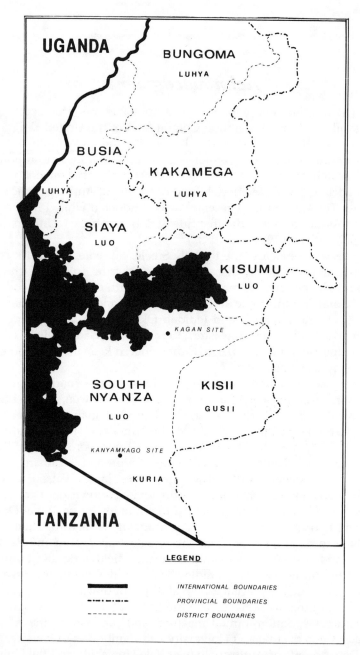

Lake Victoria region of western Kenya (Nyanza Province: Siaya, Kisumu, South Nyanza, and Kisii Districts. Western Province: Bungoma, Busia, and Kakamega Districts). [Reprinted from *Land and Society in Contemporary Africa*, by R. E. Downs and S. P. Reyna, by permission of the University Press of New England. Copyright 1988 by Trustees of the University of New Hampshire.]

1

Introduction

No society uses money in all economic exchanges. The most urban, literate, and industrial peoples offer some gifts in kind, as in rites of passage (birthdays, retirements) or gestures of diplomacy (statues, pandas). They also use specialized currencies, like food stamps, coupons, or poker chips. Barter, the direct exchange of goods without money, now accounts for a sizable part of international trade. It also occurs, and is perpetually reborn, in war-torn countries or countries with high inflation rates. These nonmonetary forms of exchange can come and go, expand and contract, as social, economic, and political circumstances change. But some rural people who have limited, tenuous contact with states, markets, and international religious and cultural traditions—those some call "peasants"—seem to hold particularly ambivalent feelings about money, and to seek ways to channel it out of special social relations.

This book is about some East African farmers, in a partly monetized economy and a partly Christianized religious environment, who have decided that there are two kinds of money, one good and one evil. Among the Kenya Luo, the classification of cash reflects important conceptual and social tensions, stemming partly from disjunctions between new kinds of private accumulation and other, indigenous forms of economic activity. Luo associate some new forms of exchange with spiritual forces, lately with the devil of Christian dogma. Money from forbidden transactions is conceived of as barren, and ultimately useless to its owner. But money is ritually transformable between good and evil states.

This much the Luo have in common with some other peoples in roughly comparable circumstances elsewhere, including some well-known cases in Latin America (Nash 1979; Taussig 1980). On both continents, distinctions between good and evil money, or its sacred and profane states, relate to recent histories of contact with foreign forms of enterprise. These beliefs and practices can be interpreted as ideological responses of poor and powerless peoples to rapid involvement

1

in market economies, and to discomforts in adjustment as inequalities widen. Some of the parallels are striking.

The Luo beliefs, however, also reflect particularly African family tensions, and they call for other special interpretations. Luo ideas about good and evil money highlight tensions arising between the sexes, and between elders and juniors, as new ways of handling family property emerge and fortunes become more volatile. The Luo beliefs about evil money are expressed in an idiom of ancestors, unilineal kin groups, and bridewealth, reflecting views of social order that the Latin American peoples discussed here do not share.

The hardest but most important questions in social science begin with "why," and this work suggests how to begin explaining the Luo concept of "bitter" or evil money, a concept apparently undocumented in previous studies available on the region. The study attempts, in the process, to say something about schools of thought in economic anthropology. It analyzes bitter money in terms of economy, politics, and culture, which I see as three primary colors for illuminating any social change. In doing so it aims to illustrate complementarity between some widely differing theories on exchange in rural Africa.

2

Understanding Ambivalence about Money in Rural Africa

A Sequence of Trends in Theory

Anthropologists today are without a commonly accepted paradigm for understanding the meaning of money in rural African life. Instead, the scene is something more like the stage floor at the end of a Shakespearean tragedy, strewn about with bleeding cadavers of actors who have slain each other one by one, lingering and overlapping in their throes.

When diffusionists began taking over center stage from evolutionists in the late 1890s, some already considered exchange and religion to be parts of the study of culture; and when Africanists like Leo Frobenius (1898) began to write of culture complexes as being transplanted from one part of the world to another, both symbols and modes of exchange could be understood to be among the possibly interwoven traits. Diffusionists of different schools in Austria, Germany, Britain, and the United States demonstrated compellingly that ways of thinking and acting can move from one people to another through travel and trade. Some got carried away, drawing arrows on maps where not all the chain links had been established. Some added strong normative judgments, or appeared to add them, so that, in the extreme arguments, "civilization" spread around the world from the Nile Valley (and then from wherever archaeologists happened to be digging up coins).[1] Unfortunately, these latter were the kinds of theories by which three decades of diffusionists would chiefly be remembered.

Their work would be judged harshly.[2] From the First World War to mid-century, British-trained structural functionalists (or just "functionalists"), influenced by Bronislaw Malinowski and A. R. Radcliffe-Brown, criticized the diffusionist and evolutionist presumptions of

19th- and early 20th-century anthropology as being pseudo-scientific, absolutist, and ethnocentric.[3] For functionalists, tracing an African belief or practice to foreign influence was to ignore its true causes: its role in the satisfaction of basic human needs (to Malinowski's followers) or in the coglike mesh of society's interdependent parts, and their equilibration (to Radcliffe-Brown and his). Missionaries and traders were viewed more as destroyers than as creators or transplanters of culture in Africa. Causal explanations like "because the Bible says so" had no important place in the proper study of mankind.[4]

By the 1960s, dependency theorists and others sternly criticized earlier functionalists for ignoring, in the search for "uncontaminated" cultures, money and other links between indigenous peoples and the outside world (though many functionalists were less guilty of this than their critics have suggested). Dependency theorists also lambasted 1950s and '60s pro-market "modernization" theorists for the ethnocentric view that the spread of cash around the world was a sign of social progress.[5] They preferred to think of cash exchanges as part of a rapelike penetration by the centers of the world economy, or the "metropolis," into the "periphery."[6]

By the early 1970s it became awkwardly apparent that "precapitalist" modes of production (and of life generally) were not universally disappearing as modernization theorists rather hoped and dependency theorists rather feared. "Marxist structuralist" theorists of the 1970s reconstrued money as part of the "articulation," or link with mutual influence, between modes of production they called precapitalist and capitalist, or part of an encapsulation of one by the other.[7] But in Africa as elsewhere, their formulations, though dazzling to many, often came up long on cumbersome terminology and short on fact. Modes, forces, and relations of production either became Procrustean beds, into which all societies and economies had to be fitted, or multiplied until, as one critic pointedly observed, "each Andean valley has its own mode of production, and individuals may change them two or three times a week like underwear" (Foster-Carter 1978:239). "Articulation" theorists lacked articulateness. Economic anthropology is now quickly retracting from this school too, and seeking a new currency: a plainer language with less ideological charge, perhaps one more receptive to ethnographic detail.

A useful legacy of 1970s "articulation" theory, however, is the acceptance that cash has entered African economies partially and unevenly, and that multiple modes of livelihood can coexist, for better or worse. Nonmarket economic behaviors—reciprocity and redistribution—are not disappearing. In Africa the chronological progression implied in terms like "capitalist" and "precapitalist" economies is too simplistic. Rather, market and nonmarket principles seem to interweave. African farmers continue to pay bridewealth in livestock or blankets, redistribute grains and meat at funerals, and share farm work reciprocally at the same time as they compete for coffee profits, speculate in land markets, or hire wage labor. No African society, before or after European times, was ever wholly socialist or capitalist, and none is likely to be soon.

But what determines where market principles apply, and where money will be used?[8]

Beyond Articulation Theory: Decision Theory and Political Economy

An attractive way of analyzing the partial acceptance of cash has arisen over the past century in the borderland between anthropology and neoclassical economics. This is the *homo rationalis* or *homo oeconomicus* approach. It is now a perennial.[9] It focuses on the individual and assumes self-interested reason, calculation, strategy. Cost-benefit analyses and decision trees are standard tools. Nonquantifiable considerations, like security or affection, have entered these models.[10] But humans in this school's view remain manipulators: they tinker with norms, structures, and perceptions for personal advantage. Money is an option weighed: an asset, for instance, more subject to inflation than livestock. Now, at least, this way of thinking is about as African as it is European, as Kenyatta has suggested in telling why he considered sheep and goats to have been "the standard currency of the Gikuyu people" of central Kenya:

> They would argue . . . that money is not a good investment, for one shilling does not bear another shilling, whereas a sheep or goat does. This, of course, is due to the ignorance of money speculation, and so they say it is better to buy a sheep or goat instead of shillings which, if buried in the ground (the only form of saving money the majority of the people know), would rot and lose their value. [1965:66][11]

Unfortunately, much of the decision-making literature neglects culture. Values, categories, and beliefs are underrepresented as decisions are traced. Humans come out looking *too* rational. Real people sometimes hear wrongly, forget, jump to conclusions, and rebel against reason. Ironically, then, decision-making models that focus on the individual are often more appropriate for studying the behavior of the aggregate. But rational individuals may aggregate into irrational collectivities, as in some African marketing cooperatives.[12] So *homo rationalis* decision theory, though powerful and promising, is not without its problems and contradictions either.

Several waves of scholarship succeeding articulation theory in the 1970s and 1980s have become known (like schools of earlier centuries) as "political economy."[13] A central feature of modern schools is their skepticism about the state, as both a political and an economic entity: more than ever, its very legitimacy is under scrutiny. The criticism is especially apt in Africa, of course, where national boundaries usually correspond not to ethnic, linguistic, or religious divisions, but instead, either to simple topographical barriers (the squiggles are rivers), or to other plainly arbitrary lines, etched with straightedges on maps by 19th-century imperial statesmen in Europe. One line separates Kenya and Tanzania, dividing Luo from Luo, Maasai from Maasai.

The political economy lens has revealed some important truths, among them, that rural Africans themselves tend to question their nations' legitimacy as units.[14] Ethnicity, assumed in much postwar scholarship to be getting homogenized in "modernization," now appears more vital than ever. Ethnic regionalism versus nationalism is, in a sense, the greatest political and economic issue in Africa south of the Sahara, both to insiders and to outsiders. It is something wars are fought over.

A skepticism applied to the state is a skepticism applied to money: to notes and coins bearing pictures of current presidents, national flags and seals, and slogans about national unity. It is a skepticism about exchange values set by finance ministries that do not correspond to exchange values in the countryside: about official rates that differ from "informal" exchange rates by a factor of ten, about inflation rates in three digits, and about currencies at times even abolished overnight. Popular responses to these seemingly capricious gyrations are governed not just by the optimizing individual "rationality" that forms the keystone of neoclassical economics and decision theory, but also by the stark facts of political instability and the collective powerlessness of rural people. To many Africans, money is something evanescent: something to get rid of before it becomes worthless. All Africanist social science sees this clearly now, under the mixed lights of politics and economics. But the political-economic human is only a two-dimensional being. There is more to social life than wealth and power. Something is missing.

And Beyond Political Economy

What is missing, often, is still culture: what is true of decision theory is also true of political economy. Customs, values, beliefs, and local social organization have not been a large part of the mainstream vocabulary stylish in 1980s Africanist social science. But to ignore culture is to ignore context. It is time, perhaps, for some "traditional" threads of anthropology, lately rather lost in the excitement over markets and states, to be woven in again. Politics, economics, and culture together—grounded where necessary in ecology, perhaps, and flecked with individual personalities—may all be needed to understand what social change is about.[15]

Some Ways Anthropologists Have Sorted Market from Nonmarket Behavior

Asking why market and nonmarket behavior appear in the same societies at once, anthropologists have tried to slice the economy in several ways. Countless studies divide populations in half: capitalist urbanites versus traditionalist country folk; ambitious, entrepreneurial juniors versus socially conscious elders; market-integrated, individualistic men versus close-knit, subsistence-oriented women; the self-aggrandizing rich versus the risk-averse, redistributive poor. Another angle is a public-private dichotomy: generosity and sharing in public, accumulation in private.[16] Or society is divided up in time and space. There are times and places for "structure," individual profit, and social distance (like weekly marketplaces), and others for "communitas" and sharing (like special groves at initiation time, or churches on sabbath days) (Turner 1969). Ethnic and religious divisions too provide convenient demarcation lines: the "minority middlemen" or "pariah capitalist" phenomenon has been studied in nearly all parts of the world.[17] Marshall Sahlins's nondualistic approach conflates kinship and residential distance on a continuum: "generalized reciprocity," "negative reciprocity," and "balanced reciprocity" marking the ends and midpoint, respectively (Sahlins 1972:191–204).[18] Money is usually expected to appear in the more marketlike transactions. Each of these schemas has been challenged in Africa—perhaps a sign that each is relevant enough to be worth qualifying.

A popular way of dividing up economic life, since about 1970, has been to distinguish levels of awareness. This mode of distinction is convenient, because it obviates the need to separate people, places, times, or particular social bonds as capitalist, noncapitalist, or in-between. Everyone has something of each within him or her. "Deconstructionism," a blend of neo-Marxist and neo-Freudian influences now in fashion, tries to peer through the cracks of superficial appearances, surfaces suspected to be socially fabricated or "constructed" to conceal disturbing truths. In a common anthropological version, culture is seen as a mask hiding or "mystifying" relations of exploitation in "false consciousness." So funerary redistributions, for instance, are an obfuscating device of culture's, hiding the facts of a land market and class polarization.[19] Monetary values for this school are a reality hidden in exploitative relations (see Bourdieu 1977:172–173): kept out of patron-client ties through gifts and payments in kind, or at least hidden in an envelope at tipping time. For money's value is too clear.

Unfortunately, the mystification approach, while useful and illuminating, sometimes raises awkward questions about who really knows what is what. "False consciousness" implies that someone has the true consciousness: the ethnographer is presumed to see more clearly, or to be less gullible or acquiescent, than the people studied. This is a weakness, a disturbing truth beneath the surface of mystification theory.

In another, more empirical vein, economic anthropologists are now looking right into African families to watch market and nonmarket behavior interact. As political economists scrutinize the state, so anthropologists are scrutinizing the household. They are finding fuzzy boundaries around the group, and competing interests, between genders and between generations, that prevent free and equal sharing of resources, or of power, within the group.[20] No longer is "the household head" considered *the* decision-maker in a family. "Income" is being reconceived as "income streams." Different kinds of wealth are seen to be controlled by different members of the household, negotiated over, and used for competing purposes.[21]

More broadly, economic anthropologists are paying more attention again to exchange and consumption, rather than just "modes of production," for social and cultural content (Appadurai 1986; Douglas and Isherwood 1978; Gregory 1982; Hart 1986). Money, exchangeable for almost anything, and variously symbolizing almost anything, provides special fascination. Testing ancient European philosophies of money in new, non-European settings, anthropologists are looking into cultural assumptions underlying perceptions of capital; for instance, constructions of money as a self-reproducing thing.[22] There is promise in this, not least for discovery or reminder of an observer's own cultural biases. Much in the ethnography remains to be done.

Substantivists like Paul Bohannan (1955, 1959) and culturally sensitive transactionalists like Fredrik Barth (1967) tried in the 1950s and early 1960s to discern local African cognitive categories for exchanges—"spheres of exchange," as Raymond Firth and others had called them in the Pacific.[23] But then the powerful wave of Lévi-Straussian structuralism in the 1960s channeled cognitive inquiry away from economic subjects toward more overtly "symbolic" topics like myth and ritual. Anthropologists are now reawakening their old concerns with the cognitive, "emic" (insiders') categories in economic life. The aims of Barth, Bohannan, and some other "economic" anthropologists were in a sense not so unlike those of the "symbolic" anthropologists who captured the limelight in anthropology. All sought to identify the cognitive categories that humans use to structure a confusing and sometimes contradictory world. Symbolics and economics need not be discrete topics. Anthropologists are now asking not only how production and other economic actions structure thought, but also how categories of thought structure economic actions.[24] All of this may help balance political economy with what one might call "cultural economy."

Bohannan (1959) has conceived of money, among the Tiv, as something that scrambles previously distinct spheres of exchange, reducing quality to quantity. The findings to be discussed here on the Kenya Luo suggest a somewhat different picture. To the extent that spheres of exchange exist among the Luo, money does not necessarily scramble the spheres. But it is usually classified as belonging to one sphere or another. How money was obtained determines how it is classed; and how it is classed determines how people think it should be used.

Sales Taboos and Purchase Taboos: Heritage Property and Other Special Property

In all societies, it seems, some goods are not deemed properly salable, including, in Europe and North America, gifts or heirlooms, things we say have "sentimental value," whether this be an accurate reason or not (and often it is not). The origin of a thing determines how it may be used or disposed of. As Arjun Appadurai (1986) and some other contributors to his volume have recently observed, goods in any society may slide in and out of commodityhood in their "lifetimes" of ownership and circulation.[25] We must ask not only why some things are sold and others not, but how and why a thing may *become* salable or unsalable.[26] And what relations might there be between sales taboos and purchase taboos?

Following an object through its "social life," in Appadurai's terms, may tell more about people than about the thing itself.[27] The

Luo of Kenya, as we shall see, follow a person's money and other wealth from acquisition to disposal. How one obtained money affects how one may dispose of it. The attachment between particular persons or groups, and particular property of special kinds, is expected not to be broken. These things may be considered special property, or perhaps *anticommodities*. When they are sold, money obtained in exchange for them becomes tainted, unusable for some other kinds of exchanges. While "special-purpose currencies" are now commonplace in the anthropological literature—special shells, brass rods, or barkcloths supposed to be exchanged for specific other kinds of goods, but not others—the Luo case presents a kind of *special-purpose cash*. Luo beliefs about tainted money link both sales taboos and purchase taboos, and not all money is freely interchangeable with other money, though of equivalent amount and appearance.

Summary

To understand the *culture* of money in the mediation of market and nonmarket relations in East Africa, then, one has a wide choice of approaches, most of which someone among us has gleefully exposed as defective in some way. Some are typically anthropological (diffusionisms, functionalisms, structuralisms, and the analysis of "spheres of exchange" combining cognitive and economic subjects). Others spring from the wider debates spanning several social sciences (modernizationist, *dependista*, "articulationist," individual decision-making, and new political-economic theories). Still others incorporate diverse strands of philosophical, psychological, and literary traditions with "critical," neo-Marxist anthropological theory (deconstructionist approaches concentrating on false consciousness or mystification).

The vehemence with which each school of thought rejects its predecessors, and especially its most immediate ones, prompts worry. Contemporary anthropological theory seeks direction.[28] Can a young discipline afford to toss out old theories with such abandon?

Analyzing a small part of a belief system discovered by chance in Kenya in the early 1980s, this study seeks to illustrate some of the ways economic and symbolic thought are linked in a quickly changing African farming society. Applying a few selected theories to the beliefs, the remaining pages draw a lesson from African thought. The need for eclecticism and tolerance in thinking about our forebears, a major part of the lesson, is not new to anthropologists, but it is one we often forget in our debates.

Notes

1. Egypto-centric diffusionists in Britain included G. Elliot Smith (see, e.g., Smith 1928) and W. J. Perry, the latter a student of W. H. R. Rivers. Other important schools of diffusionism grew up in Germany, Austria, and the United States.

2. Harris (1968: chapt. 14) surveys earlier 20th-century theories of diffusionism and some criticisms, adding a few barbs of his own. Some of the diffusionists, like W. H. R. Rivers, had in turn roundly criticized Victorian evolutionists for supposing that cultures cut off from each other could evolve in isolation.

3. Various functionalist schools of anthropological thought are concisely summarized and placed in historical context (though with different biases) in S. Barrett (1984), Harris (1968), and Kuper (1973). "Structural functionalism" is not to be confused with either "structuralism" (as Claude Lévi-Strauss represents, e.g., 1968) or with "Marxist structuralism" (articulation) theory, discussed later. Functionalist ethnographers of Africa included the young Edward Evans-Pritchard, Darryl Forde, and the South African Meyer Fortes, to name only three.

4. Even for ethnographers like Edward Evans-Pritchard and Godfrey Lienhardt, who were or became devout Christians themselves. Late in his career, Evans-Pritchard turned away from functionalism such as his now classic early works arguably exemplified, in favor of a more historical approach.

5. The broad and multistranded set of ideas now called modernization theories arose in several cross-fertilizing social sciences simultaneously after the Second World War, though they were based on evolutionary notions popular since the 19th century. Long (1977) summarizes several of the subschools concisely; for perhaps the most widely representative collection in a single volume, see Etzioni and Etzioni-Harvey (1964).

6. Long (1977: chapt. 2–4) and Robertson (1984:26–42, 48–61) compare modernization and dependency schools succinctly.

7. For succinct summaries of theoretical contributions by French and British Marxist structuralists (the "articulation of modes of production" theorists), a group almost as diverse as modernizationists or *dependistas,* see Hart (1983) and Long (1977:84–104).

8. Money is usually seen to represent market principles, and the absence of money an absence of market principles. But this may not necessarily be so. Cash sales and rentals that arise between close kin may or may not be based on market principles or prices. And barter relations, that is, those involving no money, may involve much haggling.

9. Barlett (1980) and Ortiz (1983) document and summarize varieties of formal decision-making theory in the economic anthropology of agriculture; Hill (1970, 1975) and Schneider (1974) have used it liberally in rural African studies. Central precepts derive not just from neoclassical economics, but also from a distinguished anthropological heritage including Bronislaw Malinowski, Fredrik Barth, and F. G. Bailey.

10. The 1960s saw a rather overpolarized debate between "formalists," who supposed neoclassical economics to be universally applicable, and "substantivists," some of them followers of Karl Polanyi, who thought not. LeClair and Schneider (1968) contains articles representing both sides.

11. Kenyatta, the first President of Kenya who was to keep the country on the pro-market course charted by its British rulers, had lived and studied in Britain before writing *Facing Mount Kenya*. His prose clearly reflects some European as well as Kikuyu ideas about investment. But similar arguments about cash are heard in many parts of Africa where livestock are kept. See, for example, Malcolm (1938, vol. II:128) on Sukuma cattle-owners of Tanzania, who said, *shilingi jitobialaga* (shillings don't breed). Schneider (1974:172–175) takes a formalist argument to an extreme in contending that among the Turu and other East Africans, cattle *are* money by several definitions.

12. A common pattern is that farmers borrow from their local cooperatives on the promise to repay by selling their products back to the cooperative. But each farmer acts in his or her own self-interest, and sells to some third party instead. The cooperative fails, and all the farmers in it ultimately lose by the "rational" behavior of each one. Game theories may be used to help understand situations like this.

13. "Political economy" can mean almost anything to anybody. From Sir James Steuart in the late 18th century through John Stuart Mill in the mid-19th, it tended to mean economics generally; now it often means critical social studies (including Marxist sorts), as in the journal, *Review of African Political Economy* or Saul and Arrighi (1973). In literature on development in Africa, Robert Bates's influential work (1983) represents a kind of neoclassical, populist variant of political economy; Bunker (1986) and Hart (1982) blend in more cultural and social anthropology. In a discussion spanning several social sciences, several centuries, and several continents, Hart (1986) discusses theories on money as a token of authority, and as a commodity with a price; ambivalence about money is a central concept throughout.

14. The political economy of the 1980s has sometimes oversimplified, however, in dichotomizing "people" and "the state." Some rural Africans identify more closely with their nations than others, and loyalties waver. All statesmen and stateswomen are people; and many have their own rural interests at stake as well as urban ones. In Africa, the dichotomy can be as deceptive as those between modern and traditional, or between precapitalist and capitalist modes of livelihood. Among studies of Africa and other parts of the world, Bunker (1986), Clastres (1977), Grindle (1986), and Robertson (1984) all present more complex analyses of relations between "people" (or "Society") and "the state" than their dichotomous titles might suggest on the surface.

15. Berry (1985), Hart (1982), and Murray (1981) are among the bravest attempts yet to synthesize the three disciplines in the study of rural Africa. All incidentally combine neoclassical and Marxist economic influences.

16. As in Parkin's *Palms, Wine, and Witnesses* (1972), tellingly subtitled *Public Spirit and Private Gain in an African Farming Community*; another, North African example is Bourdieu (1977).

17. African studies inspired by Weber's *Protestant Ethic and the Spirit of Capitalism* (1958) have emphasized the specially entrepreneurial and individ-

ualistic tendencies of particular minority sects (e.g., Jehovah's Witnesses in Zambia in Long (1968); Muslims in coastal Kenya in Parkin (1972)). Iliffe (1983) offers a comparative historical survey. Literature reviews and bibliographies on the "pariah capitalist" phenomenon worldwide appear in Bonacich and Modell (1980) and in the journal *Ethnic Groups*.

18. So simple and convenient, Sahlins's theory of generalized, balanced, and negative reciprocity has become a central and indispensable idea in economic anthropology. But not many realize how many transactions around the world contravene the rule. A few of them are the seemingly ubiquitous African and Latin custom of the marketplace vendor's adding a free handful of food on completing a sale, the "silent trade" that has sometimes occurred between members of hostile ethnic groups in Africa (including, it is said, Luo and Maasai in the late 19th century), and the classic Trobriand *kula* and Northwest coast potlatch. All these cases involve generalized, or at least balanced, reciprocity between partners who may be unconnected by kinship or neighborhood, and who are potentially hostile. Some, notably the market-vendors' gifts, may be construed as "mystifying" gestures concealing the true, self-interested nature of the exchange relation.

19. Parkin (1972, 1978) and Bourdieu (1977) use mystification theory to good effect in rural Africa; the first at least was published before the term "deconstruction" came into common use. Both ethnographers treat levels of awareness and the public-private distinction together; Parkin (1972) adds age and religious dimensions for a many-sided view of individual decisions in a process of class stratification among the coastal Girirama of Kenya; Parkin (1978) treats Luo in Nairobi. Taussig (1980), discussed below, is an example of Marxist deconstruction anthropology, building also on "articulation" theory.

20. Some of these ideas are old, in African anthropology, but they have been taken seriously in other disciplines only after being championed by some of the French "Marxist structuralist" anthropologists (Pierre-Philippe Rey, Georges Dupré) and later, in different ways, by a wave of guardedly feminist economic anthropologists and others these have influenced in turn (Berry 1985; Guyer 1981; Hill 1975; Moock 1986 and contributors therein; Whitehead 1981). A hallmark of most of these latter authors is their criticism of dualistic writings by their predecessors, about families or other subjects: for example, dichotomies like modern/traditional, micro/macro, or cash economy/subsistence economy. Implicit sometimes is a rejection of Lévi-Straussian structuralism, with its heavy emphasis on binary opposition.

21. Here as elsewhere, some of the lessons are rediscoveries. See, for instance, Field (1940:54–57) on the Ga peoples of Ghana, for findings about sharp divisions of resources between husbands and wives, now a topic deemed as hot as any. But the work done now is no less interesting.

22. Countless European classics, as diverse as Aristotle's *Politics* (book 1, chapt. 9), Shakespeare's *Timon of Athens* (act IV, scene 3, lines 26–45), and Marx's early writings (1970:603–604) and *Capital* (vol. I, parts I and II), remark upon the moral confusions money can bring by letting humans scramble use value with exchange value, means with ends. These three authors share a view of money's morality as "unnatural." See Taussig (1980) and Appadurai (1986) for contemporary anthropological applications of Marx's notion of "commodity fetishism." Taussig begins his argument with a vehement rejection of evolutionist modernization theory.

23. The intellectual history of "spheres of exchange," and their spread from Pacific islands to Africa in the anthropological literature, is a microcosm of diffusion. Discrete categories of transfer had been explored since the First World War or earlier in Melanesia, where they were sometimes designated by other terms. Malinowski's famous Trobriand *kula* (1922) was an early example. Firth's description of exchange categories among the Polynesian Tikopia summed up the theory: "There are at least three separate series of exchanges, or spheres of exchange, the goods in which are not completely convertible into those of the other series": the food series, the bark-cloth sinnet series, and the bonito-hook, turmeric, and canoe series. . . . "It is impossible for example to express the value of a bonito-hook in terms of a quantity of food, since no such exchange is ever made and would be regarded by the Tikopia as fantastic." A possible fourth sphere, according to Firth, included women and land, "given in satisfaction of unique obligations; they are alike in that their productive capacity is vast but incalculable!" (Firth 1967 [1939]:340, 344). Karl Polanyi's work on market and nonmarket exchange in Europe (1944) also inspired Bohannan (1955), who perceived among the Tiv of northern Nigeria three spheres, including a special bridewealth sphere, and distinguished "conveyance," exchanges within spheres, from the less common "conversion," exchanges between. Barth (1967), writing on Darfur in Sudan, added the insight that crossing spheres (making Firth's "fantastic" exchange) was what made entrepreneurs, and what made them succeed (see also Douglas and Isherwood 1978:131–132; Gudeman 1986:122–128; Schneider 1974:168–175). Gudeman discusses reinterpretations of exchange spheres by neoclassicists, substantivists, and Marxists.

24. Gudeman's *Economics as Culture* argues, "economies and economic theories are social constructions. The central processes of making a living are culturally modeled . . . among many non-Western peoples these constructions of livelihood are metaphors or extended metaphors" (1986:vii).

25. Luo diviners sometimes keep coins as one of many kinds of small objects they toss onto a flat surface to read for signs on behalf of their clients. This is money out of circulation as currency, in this sense like an American shopkeeper's first earned dollar bill, framed for the wall, or a coin in a piece of jewelry.

26. This is not, of course, a wholly new idea. Over a century ago, an informant of James G. Swan on Prince of Wales Island, off the northwest coast of Canada, illustrated nicely how the social history of a thing, rather than its inherent nature, determines its salability. Silver-laden and on a buying spree for the Smithsonian Institution in 1875, Swan found he could buy almost anything, including the largest canoe in the region. All the Northwest Coast inhabitants refused to sell was the beautifully carved columns in their villages. The local explained, "These posts are monuments for the dead and we will not sell them any more than white people will sell the grave stones or monuments in cemeteries but you can have one made for you" (Swan's diary, quoted in Doig 1980:157). A century before that, in a wholly different setting, Samuel Johnson gave this advice to a friend: "An ancient estate should always go to males. It is mighty foolish to let a stranger have it. . . . As for an estate newly acquired by trade, you may give it, if you will, to the dog *Towser*" (quoted in Boswell 1917 [1792]).

27. Appadurai's approach in economic anthropology is paralleled by an approach some agricultural economists in Michigan State University are now promoting, which they call "subsector analysis" (see, for instance, Boomgard et al. 1986). This involves following a commodity longitudinally from raw materials to consumer, to identify the constraints on its production and distribution. Both approaches spring from a contemporary concern with process through time.

28. S. Barrett (1984) and Ortner (1984) survey the scene, sharing views of many other anthropologists.

3

The Luo: Background

After 70 years under British rule and 25 more within the margins of a pro-Western, pro-enterprise state, the two million Luo (or Joluo) of the Nyanza Province of Kenya are well familiar with, though not wholly absorbed in, market economy.[1] They are also partially integrated into an international religious tradition. The conflicts they are witnessing between local and supralocal cultures are enormous, and the decisions they are facing, momentous. The following few pages sketch some of the main features of their society, suggesting the weave of change and continuity that colors their lives today, and their ambivalence toward exogenous novelty. Beliefs about money then come into focus as a central point of debate, and for the outsider, as one way of understanding the Luo world.

Having moved over the past 450 to 500 years (Crazzolara 1950:31–32; Ogot 1967:28–41) from the Bahr el Ghazal region of the Sudan, where their cousins the Nuer and Dinka now live, the Kenya Luo live in a densely settled land of separated farmsteads in three districts around the eastern shore of Lake Victoria, an area now rather loosely webbed with roads. The landscape changes from flat and dry by the lake, to green and hilly in the eastern uplands. Occupying a unified territory, from close to the Uganda border in the northwest into Tanzania in the south, the Luo are fairly homogeneous in language, and their communities are interlinked throughout by marriage and other kin ties. Luo have market contacts with members of several neighboring groups, though some of the boundaries are considered sharp. Clockwise from the north on a map, their neighbors are the Luhya, Nandi, Gusii, Maasai, and Kuria.[2] They also have dealings with immigrant Indian, Middle Eastern, and Somali traders in the towns of the region. These groups are endogamous, and while rural Luo depend on them for provisions, the relations between the majority and minorities are generally cool. The provincial capital, Kisumu, connects by rail and air to Nairobi.

Livelihood, Politics, and Egalitarian Ideology

Rural Luo cobble together their livelihood from many activities, on and off the farm, and many have several "occupations" simultaneously. With ox-plows and hand hoes they grow maize, sorghum, millet, and many other vegetable foods, and several cash crops including coffee, sugarcane, tobacco, cotton, and groundnuts, depending on altitude and rainfall, soils, and access to markets. They also herd cattle—cherished animals still used for bridewealth payments among other things—and sheep and goats, and raise chickens; some also fish in the lake and streams. For about fifty years, about a third of the middle-aged men have lived outside the Luo homeland at any given time in their search for wage labor either in Kenya's plantations, towns, and cities, or in other countries of East Africa (see Parkin 1978; Stichter 1982; Whisson 1964). Within Nyanza Province, several large sugar plantations established under Asian management early in the century, and one from the late 1970s, provide some manual jobs, mostly "casual." Rural families depend on members' labor migrations for remittances in cash and kind, but migrants also depend on rural farms as safety nets, sources of occasional food, and eventual retirement homes.

The Luo see themselves as an egalitarian people. While inequalities in wealth show up clearly in Luo neighborhoods—tin roofs among thatched roofs, motor vehicles among pedestrians, pressed shirts among tattered rayon ones and bare chests—the Luo are known for, and proud of, their leveling ideology.[3] In a well-known anecdote, Oginga Odinga, the aging former Vice President (of Jomo Kenyatta) whom many still see as the great Luo patriarch, has reminisced of a famine in his youth, during which his father's brother sneaked about at night to the granaries of local families, to even out supplies (Odinga 1967:7). In times of plenty, Luo children given snack food can be seen dividing it out equally to others present, silently and unhesitatingly (a marvel to some foreign visitors). The egalitarian ethos underlies redistributive behavior of many kinds: contributions to weddings, bridewealth, and funerals, interfamilial livestock loans and school fee payments, reciprocal labor exchanges, and lately, rotating savings and loan clubs and other self-help groups. Of course, the same mechanisms can be used for personal accumulation too, but it is always advantageous to appear, at least, to be a sharer. Fears of witchcraft accusations, gossip, and general ostracism check fast grabbing and ostentation: getting rich too quickly subjects a Luo to rumors about cattle thievery or worse sins like father-beating. Beliefs about "bitter money" will be seen to reflect similar concerns.

Politically, too, egalitarian principles figure importantly in Luo life. In precolonial times the Luo had not a unified political structure, but a system of local leaders with rather weak and sometimes only semiformal positions (a point sometimes debated) at the head of exogamous clans or maximal lineage federations (sing. *oganda*, pl. *ogendni* or *ogendini*).[4] The territories of these are now administered as "locations" with chiefs under the national government. There was no great hierarchic bureaucracy as in interlacustrine kingdoms of Uganda. Patrilineal kinship and clanship, and the cross-cutting marriage ties, were the main stitching holding Luo society together; in the 20th century churches and various kinds of voluntary associations have also played an increasing role in social organization.

Partly because their political system was not structurally receptive to the colonially imposed hierarchy of provincial, district, and divisional officers and local chiefs, but also because of Luo people's separate cultural and linguistic identity as western Nilotes, many Luo prefer a certain measure of political autonomy. A century of superficially peaceful integration into Kenya has masked some tensions, particularly between the Luo and the Bantu-speaking Kikuyu of central Kenya, but also at times between the Luo and the colonial and postcolonial governments. The Luo have a history of rocky relations with agricultural and other "extension" agents from outside, many of whom have variously misunderstood the ecological and social systems of Nyanza Province (see Butterman 1979; Hay 1972; Lonsdale 1964; Shipton 1985). Ethnic tensions have intertwined with political and economic disagreements as Oginga Odinga and his followers have voiced general discontents in leftward-leaning speeches and at times been punished.[5]

Odinga's "purist" Luo traditionalism had a counterpoint in the urban, pro-market orientation of the second most prominent Luo leader, Tom Mboya, until the latter's assassination in 1969 (see Goldsworthy 1982; Parkin 1978:217–242). Mboya tended to think this way:

> Among the economic changes that planning must bring about is the conversion of the subsistence sectors of our economies into market economies. . . . This requires not only trust in others but trust in the economic system itself. . . . The use of money as a medium of exchange is closely related to our desire to develop a market economy. . . . Money is clearly an established institution which will make easier our task of introducing other economic institutions. [T. Mboya 1970:176–177]

Odinga and Mboya led a national party split and today's active Luo politicians still play out a resonant dialectic of their own within the new one-party state. The two men's competing images symbolize Luo ambivalence about change. But Kenyans have constructed the dominant image of the Luo as closet separatists and closet socialists. However exaggerated or oversimplified, the stereotype feeds back into young Luo minds and may be pushing along a tradition itself.

Kinship, Gender, and Age

Luo political organization ties directly into relations of kinship, gender, and age. The Luo are a classic case, and one of the best available, of a segmentary lineage society (Evans-Pritchard 1965; Goldenberg 1982; Parkin 1978; Shipton 1984a, 1984b; Southall 1952). This means that kin groups based on real or putative descent through one sex, in this case male, divide and subdivide like branches of a tree. Patronymic in naming, virilocal in postmarital residence, and, in a third of the family homesteads, polygynous, the Luo give a high public profile to males. Patriliny, bridewealth, and polygyny all reinforce each other.[6]

Reproduction is a key underlying concern. It is a basis of the value system by which men judged exchanges in the past, in a pattern, locally called *rundo* (or turning around), familiar elsewhere in Africa. As a Luo informant characteristically told Judith Butterman, "That was the big trade in the past: cultivation to chickens, chickens to goats, goats to cows; cows to women" (1979:61).[7] With women, children: hands to cultivate. As discussed later, Luo believe that misusing money can cause human and animal infertility—for them the worst fate imaginable.

Fertility is at least as much a woman's as a man's anxiety, for women's social status and marriages depend on their producing offspring. *Ogendni* or clans being exogamous, however, women live their married lives as only partial members of their husbands' kin groups. As immigrants from all over Luoland (and occasionally from outside) living among interrelated men, the married women of a locality lack the convenient framework of social and political organization that men make of lineages.

Gender charts the possibilities of a Luo's economic life. Wives keep separate houses within the circular homesteads of the larger polygynous families, and they farm separate fields and granaries, but men are normally considered the *weg dala* (sing. *wuon dala*), homestead heads, and they reserve both symbolic and practical rights over homestead property. Husbands and wives tend to do separate farm tasks, the women doing the most time-consuming work on the basic staples, the men taking more interest in the cash crops or food crops to be marketed in bulk, and generally doing less of the farm work than women. Both men and women frequent the rural marketplaces that have become a central feature of western Kenyan life in the past century, but here too, women specialize in smaller-scale trading. While many husbands try to control their wives' incomes, spouses do not always share money with each other, or the knowledge of how much they possess.

Age is deeply respected, as in much of East Africa. Although the Luo have no formal age-grade system like those of the neighboring Maasai, Nandi, or Kuria, their society could be called a gerontocracy, at least until lately. Elder men have controlled the allocation of bridewealth cattle, land, and to an extent, labor. They also seek to control the cash, and a young man with a salary or wage may find his father demands a good part of it straight off. In Luo ideology, age, wealth, and respect come together, and it is considered natural that elders—*jodongo* or "big ones"—should control family resources. They sit in the central positions in chiefs' meetings, command family obedience, and are broadly referred to as repositories of wisdom. Elder men are also considered the natural representatives of their families to the outside world. Luo gerontocratic tendencies rely partly on the nearness of elders to the ancestors and ancestorhood. This brings us to religion and spiritual cosmology.

Religion: Overlaps and Admixtures of Old and New

In religion, education, and some other aspects of culture, Christian mission influences in Luoland and environs have been heavy, making for a rich and complex mixture of old and new.[8] The scant available evidence on the Luo in precolonial Kenya suggests their religious tradition included a high god (or at least creator and life force) Nyasaye or Were, manifested in the sun and extraordinary earthly things. Ancestral and other spirits were, and still remain, active forces in local conceptions of the world. Luo refer to spirits by the terms *tipo* (pl. *tipo*), or shadow; *juok* (pl. *juogi*), generally, spiritual force; and *kwaro* (pl. *kwere*), grandfather or earlier agnatic forebear; and various other terms, depending on the locality and context, the type and behavior of the spirit, and the use of euphemism.[9] They identify spirits with male or female ancestors, and pay most attention to those of people who were somehow important when alive, or who are related in particularly important ways to the living concerned. Ancestors in the male line usually are the most respected and feared. People perceive spirits as agents of good, evil, or both. They may see, hear, feel, or smell them, or see them in their dreams. They also sense their presence in their own turns of fortune, including those involving money. Spirits watch some money more than other money, as we shall see, and beliefs in spirits may cause humans to worry, to sacrifice, to debate, and sometimes to change their minds about how to spend.

Sudden gains and losses in life also call into play Luo beliefs in witchcraft and magic of benevolent and malevolent sorts, practiced by men or women. These beliefs persist, some in changing forms, despite strong challenges from churches and schools. Concepts corresponding to witchcraft or magic are denoted by *juok* (pl. *juogi*), *bilo*, (pl. *bilo*), *nawi* (pl. *nepe*), and numerous other terms, again, depending on the locality, the intention, the agency, and the kinds of objects or substances manipulated, if any.[10] Some powers of witchcraft or magic are considered inherited, others learned. Divination, like liquor brewing, can be a profitable part-time occupation for some rural women, who may have few other better sources of income.

Since before the turn of the 20th century, British, American, and other Catholic and Protestant missions have competed for converts in the Luo country, the strongest churches carving up the region sharply into hegemonic territories smaller than districts.[11] The Seventh-Day Adventist mission was set up in 1906, and by 1913, the Gospel According to St. Matthew was translated into Luo (Butterman 1979:127). Mission churches entered Kenya and have remained under the umbrella of government, but have also occasionally operated at loggerheads with government in roles of public advocacy. They have organized numerous "development" initiatives of many kinds. Some churches have profoundly influenced local education in establishing mission schools, which, among other things, have served and molded local elites; and Luo have taken advantage of the chances more generally in forming a kind of ethnic intellectual elite in Kenya.[12]

In addition to foreign-based missions, countless and diverse independent African Christian churches have appeared since the first, the Nomiya Luo Church, began in 1914.[13] Most of the independent African churches in western Kenya have begun as direct or indirect offshoots of particular foreign churches, and many of the larger ones have sprouted separatist churches themselves. The Luo and nearby Luhya and Gusii peoples are becoming noted in theological circles throughout the Christian world for the number and strength of these groups.

The local independent churches' way of continually dividing and subdividing reflects in some way the ramifying segmentary lineage system that is such an important part of Luo, Luhya, and Gusii life. In a sense, churches over time seem to constitute a kind of alternative or shadow lineage system. Church membership is not, however, coterminous with lineage membership. Often it crosscuts it, and some churches seem constituted mainly along lines of matrilateral and affinal kinship. Married women sometimes rely on church ties to help compensate for lack of full membership in their husbands' patrilineages.

More broadly, many independent churches may be understood partly as political or quasi-political movements as well as religious ones.[14] If Luo have no chance or unified desire for political independence—and their sentiments are much more mixed than this—some can at least declare independence from broader religious hierarchies and substitute structures of their own, hierarchical or not.

Taken together, Christianity as foreign missionaries conceive of it has only partly eradicated indigenous Luo religion. The traditions of thought and practice found today in the region weave together local and exogenous strands, in a variegated fabric not devoid of stresses and strains. Indigenous and exogenous marriage systems, methods of praise and prayer, food and drink taboos, and dress codes all interthread, but not in a static or homogeneous way. Individuals who find that the strictures of their churches do not fit their habits or ambitions—for example, monogamists who become interested in plural marriage, or drinkers who wish to quit drinking—commonly switch to sects that fit their needs or ambitions more closely. In the choices among beliefs there is some syncretism. Though missionaries have tried hard to stamp out ancestral spirits, these remain active in the minds of many Luo who worship Christ and the Christian deity.

Money

Money as coinage or printed notes has been in general use in the Luo country only since the turn of the 20th century: it came at about the same time as the Bible. Most of Luoland lay well away from the major long-distance trade routes of the 19th century. Although Luo knew specialized or "intermediate" currencies like iron wire *(nalo)* for arm or leg bands, and doubtless some knew money too, before the establishment of the British East Africa Protectorate in 1895, it was the colonial impetus that first caused money's spread, and Luo have always associated it with alien authority while finding it convenient for their own purposes.[15]

British colonial "hut" (i.e., house) taxes, first required under the Native Administration Ordinance of 1900, and collected through newly installed chiefs, forced Luo to earn money. Since each married woman normally had one house, the tax was effectively a tax on women. It was often women who had to pay it, and at first, many did so in the form of iron wire or a goatskin rather than the one to two rupees (Butterman 1979:124–125).[16] Within the next few years, cotton and other cash crops were introduced, the Uganda Railway was built, and settler farms were established requiring Kenyan wage labor.[17]

Five years later, when the annual hut tax was three rupees, new colonial administrators were already noting, as one so ethnocentrically wrote of the Luo, "a surprising quickness to learn the lessons of civilisation, e.g., their ready change from trade goods to cash in commercial matters" (Northcote 1907:66). Soon children too were involved in the cash economy, on a small scale. South Nyanza District Commissioner Hunter wrote these remarks about a tour of schools in 1936, revealing, again, as much about colonial administration as about local habits:

> At one outschool, a sector school all the pupils were paraded for my inspection in Khaki uniform and red fez caps. On enquiry I learnt that the boys had purchased these themselves with money obtained from the sale of groundnuts and cotton in their school gardens. We want very much more of this kind of education. . . . I find that quite apart from the combined cotton patches, many of the children have small areas from which they derive a little pocket money. The parents in most cases allow them to keep this and they buy a pair of shorts or such like. . . . A further point that struck me on the safari was that at each of the subsidiary camps I was asked to partake of tea and found a well set out tea table and in one case sweet scones provided. It was on the whole a truly enlightening safari into the gradual social advance of the natives of this area.[18]

An ethnographer studying the Luo northwest of Kisumu town in the late 1940s noted that metal ornaments as trade currency were then a thing of the past (Waligorski 1970:19). Barter was still seen, though cash seemed to be increasingly supplanting it too.[19]

Today no Luo can do without money. Clothes, schooling, and local and Western medical care all cost money. Salt, sugar, cooking oil, and matches are ubiquitous purchased goods. All the crops the Luo grow, and all the animals they raise, are sold at least on occasion; and several of the newer crops, including cotton, coffee (from mid-century), and sunflowers (being introduced now) are sold almost exclusively for cash. Where barter occurs, in Luoland, both parties usually have monetary values of the goods or services in mind.

As "intermediate currency," as minted tender, or as credit, money tends to free an African farmer from depending on the elements or the goodwill of his or her neighbors, for food and other provisions each year. Saved in padlocked boxes, mattresses, and by a few men, in banks, money can buy a Luo what might otherwise require cooperation.[20] People with money can live by different rules than people without. Luo who will lend neighbors farm tools or lanterns freely may refuse to lend cash: it is harder to collect. Nothing is more sought after than cash, but nothing disappears more quickly. Cash has created its own morality.

But money has not taken over all transactions and is unlikely to do so soon. Farmers continue to engage in permanent or temporary local contracts exchanging land, labor, and livestock directly—to name only three factors of production (Johnson 1980; Shipton 1985; cf. Robertson 1987). Rural Luo now pay bridewealth in livestock, though they supplement this with cash (cf. Parkin 1980). Kin appearing at funerals present the immediate family of the dead with grain or other edibles; only those living too far to come are likely to send money instead. Household guests bring gifts like tea, sugar, or clothes, but not money. As everywhere, exchanges in kind are warmer and more personal than those with cash.[21] Money creeps into most kinds of transactions, but in some, the Luo discernibly try to keep it out.

The Luo remain acutely conscious of what they see as their past, jealously guarding what remains of their cultural, political, and economic independence. To the accelerating pace of change their responses remain deeply ambivalent. It is this ambivalence, and the attempts to reconcile ideals with actions, that their current beliefs about bitter money may serve to illustrate.

Notes

1. Kenya is divided administratively into provinces, districts, divisions, locations, and sublocations. The Luo comprise the great majority of the populations of three districts in Nyanza Province: Siaya, Kisumu, and South Nyanza. In the Luo language (dhoLuo), prefixes can denote person. *Jaluo* thus refers to one Luo, *Joluo* to more than one.

2. Some groups of Luo-speakers of Bantu origins, called Suba, live in parts of South Nyanza District, including its islands. Culturally they are almost fully assimilated. South of the Luo in Tanzania live Kuria and Jita groups.

3. For more on Luo egalitarian ideals, see Goldenberg (1982:137–140), P. Mboya (1938), Ocholla-Ayayo (1976:242, 236–239), Odinga (1967:1–14), Parkin (1978:92–98), Shipton (1985), Waligorski (1970:20), and Whisson (1962b:7, 1964:44–45).

4. Orthography of Luo terms in this study follows standard English-alphabet listings in the dictionaries of Blount and Blount (n.d.) and Stafford (1967); terms unlisted are given spellings conventional in South Nyanza District. Ogot (1967) argues that Luo leaders held hereditary offices.

5. Odinga's autobiography (1967) gives an introduction; for the patient, the Kenya *Weekly Review* and Nairobi newspapers of the 1970s and '80s document the raging verbal wars and house arrests of Odinga's aging years. As Parkin suggests (1978:220), the Kenya People's Union, the party Odinga founded in 1966, is sometimes portrayed as being more left-wing than is easy to demonstrate. Odinga's son, Raila Odinga, has recently been in and out of detention in Kenya, accused of allegedly subversive designs or activities.

6. A central argument of Parkin (1978). For other examinations of Luo bridewealth, see also Ocholla-Ayayo (1979), Parkin (1980), and Wilson (1961).

7. *Rundo* (v.t.) also means to rotate, to sell crops for money, or to confuse or mislead. This combination of meanings hints that crops and money—and perhaps the other commodities—may belong to ideally separate spheres, but the evidence is not conclusive.

8. Whisson (1964) broadly describes changes in Luo religion up to then; Hauge (1974) and Ocholla-Ayayo (1976), Luo ethics and indigenous spiritual life generally, and Evans-Pritchard (1950) and Abe (1978), some Luo beliefs and practices concerning ancestral spirits.

9. Terms for spirits include *tipo* (pl. *tipo*), shade or shadow, a term often used for the spirits of the newly dead, as in funerals; *juok* or *juogi*, (pl. *juogi*), also used in the singular for the supreme being, or in other contexts meaning witchcraft—*juogi* also means possession by a spirit; *jakwath* (pl. *jokwath*), guardian spirit or herdsman; *jachien* (pl. *jochiende*), an unhappy spirit or demon that haunts or troubles; or *jagunda* (pl. *jogunda*), one that inhabits an abandoned homestead site. *Chuny* (pl. *chuny*) means liver or sometimes heart, but also the spirit or soul, often used of the living. In the past, particular animals or inanimate objects were also associated with spirits.

10. Some concepts corresponding to "witchcraft" or "magic" are *juok* (pl. *juogi*), witchcraft, also an inherited name; *nawi* (pl. *nepe*), poison, magic, or spell; *bilo* (pl. *bilo*), medicine, often powder and usually protective; and *yath* (pl. *yien, yiedhe*), medicine or poison; *manyasi*, a solution of medicinal herbs and water; and *ndagla*, evil magic using an offensive object. The standard prefix *ja* (pl. *jo*) is used to refer to one who manipulates spiritual forces. Thus *ajuoga* (pl. *ajuoge, ajuoke*), from *juok*, is a broadly used term meaning diviner, witch, or medicine man or woman; a *jadil* (pl. *jodil*—from *dilo*, cleansing ritual) is a specialist in spirits or ghosts. *Japuok* (pl. *jopuok*) refers to a night runner or a woman with the power of the evil eye which causes internal illness; this power is called *sihoho* and is thought to belong only to some women.

11. In the parts of South Nyanza District where most of the fieldwork for this study was done, the strongest foreign-based church is the Seventh-Day Adventist Church, which started work in what is now Nyanza Province in 1906. The Kenya SDA church is part of the East African Union of SDAs; the mother SDA church is headquartered in Washington, D.C. Anglicans of the Church of the Province of Kenya (CPK), Diocese of Maseno South, carry on the tradition imported to the Lake Victoria Basin in the late decades of the 19th century by missionaries of the London-based Church Missionary Society. Also strong is the (Roman) Catholic Church in Kenya, founded upon the local establishment of the London-based Mill Hill Fathers, who also first began proselytizing in the region in the late 19th century. Other foreign-based churches

active in the area include those of Pentecostal Evangelists and the Salvation Army.

12. Some consider the Luo dominance in Kenya's intellectual scene a response to a lack or loss of economic and political power, or a kind of holding pattern.

13. The oldest independent African church sect in Nyanza is Nomiya Luo Church, formed as the Nomiya Luo Mission in 1914 as the first independent African church in Kenya, and headquartered now in Kisumu. Its founder was the prophet Johana Owalo, who had catechized under the Catholic, Seventh-Day Adventist, and Anglican missions. (An offshoot church much smaller in membership is the Nomiya Luo Sabbath, founded in 1957, partly influenced by Islam, and based in Nairobi.) Other especially important independent churches in the Luo country are the following: the Maria Legio of Africa, a female-founded church dating from the early 1960s, headquartered in South Nyanza, and mixing elements of Catholicism and indigenous Luo practice; the African Israel Church Nineveh, founded in 1942 from Canadian Pentecostalist roots, and based north of Kisumu; and several churches using the name Roho (spirit) or Roho Maler (Holy Spirit), including the Roho Church of God in Israel, founded in 1963 by a former Pentecostalist as the African Spiritual Israel Church and renamed twice later in the decade; and the Roho mar Nyasaye Mission (Spirit of God Mission). For basic information on these and other Kenyan independent churches, see D. Barrett et al. (1973), an annotated directory; Whisson (1964); and Wipper (1977). A doctoral dissertation being completed by Nancy Schwartz of Princeton University treats the Maria Legio Church in Nyanza on the basis of intensive observation.

14. Fernandez (1978) and Ranger (1986) review a broad literature on the connections between religious and political movements in Africa south of the Sahara. See Temu (1972) on the early 20th-century activities of Protestant missions in Kenya, and Whisson (1964:111–181) on independent African churches among the Luo.

15. Money is defined here as serving at least several of the following purposes: a medium of exchange, a standard of value, a store of value or wealth, a standard of deferred payment, or a unit of account. For discussions of these and other definitions see Neale (1976), Simmel (1978), and Weber (1947:172–181, 280–309).

16. Rupees are no longer in use. Today the Kenyan currency is the shilling; 20 are informally called a pound.

17. Early taxation in Nyanza is discussed in Butterman (1979), Fearn (1961), Hay (1972:122), Kitching (1980:25, 29), and Lonsdale (1964).

18. K. L. Hunter, safari diary, 3–4, December 1936, Administrative Reports ADM 12/4/1 (3/2019) Nyanza D.C., Syracuse University Microfilms 2800, reel 279; quoted in Butterman (1979:164).

19. Northcote (1907:58), Waligorski (1970:19), and Whisson (1962a:13) discuss early 20th-century "intermediary" currencies like iron wire, brass rings, and hoes, and standards of measurement and value like grain baskets of graduated sizes. For information on barter in mid-century, see these sources and Wagner (1956, vol. II:161–162). Substitutions of cash for other exchange media

are not necessarily irreversible, as the temporary use of petroleum fuels or cigarettes as currency in parts of war-torn Uganda in recent decades demon-
strates. Compare Humphrey (1985) on Southern Asian barter.

20. Margaret Field (1940:217) wrote of the Ga of Ghana, "The first step in
the loss of the sense of togetherness was the coming of money. Money could
buy you food and make you independent of the yearly gifts of the earth and
the help of relatives. Its possession did not depend on goodness—rather it was
the contrary." The functionalist cast of her words was distinctly 20th century,
but the basic idea can be found in John Locke's second treatise of government
(1960 [1689], sect. 50; see also MacPherson 1962:208–209).

21. See Parkin (1980). Perhaps a similar sentiment is reflected, too, in the
English expression "cold cash."

4

Bitter Money

Pesa makech is a term Luo use to describe ill-gotten money.[1] *Pesa* is money; anglophone Luo commonly translate *makech* in this context as "bitter," but the word can mean other things at the same time: biting, nasty, cruel, evil, dangerous.[2] A near English equivalent is "dirty money," but this idea does not capture the spiritual dimensions of the Luo concept, or the restrictions the Luo place on the money's uses.[3]

Bitter money is a special instance of what Luo sometimes call *gueth makech,* best translated as "bitter blessings" or "bitter rewards." These are benefits deriving from unfair or unjust activities, and therefore unable to help one in the long run. The "bitterness" is figurative. How one has gained a reward determines whether or how one should use it. Luo pay special attention to money.

To the Luo, bitter money is dangerous to its holder and the holder's family, because of its associations with spirits, and, in the minds of some Luo, with divinity. It must be kept strictly apart from transactions involving permanent lineage wealth and welfare, notably from livestock or bridewealth transactions.

Money obtained in several ways is thought bitter. One way is by "windfall," unearned gain: finding someone's lost money, or winning a lottery. Another is by a reward for killing or hurting others, as with a hired criminal or (according to some) a mercenary soldier. Theft is another source of bitter money, dangerous to its spender. This money is rather like stolen food, which the Luo, like some other East Africans, warn themselves not to eat for fear it will harm them.[4] The danger or "bitterness" in bitter money does not follow it as it circulates, but sticks with the one who procured it by misdeed. The "spirit of the gift" is here inverted. Bitter money contains instead something one might call the "spirit of the theft."[5]

Most commonly, though, bitter money comes from sales. In southern Luoland there are several commodities normally thought to yield the seller bitter money. These include land, gold, tobacco, and cannabis. Many also say that selling a homestead rooster will produce money that is bitter. These material things are not necessarily considered evil or dangerous in themselves. What makes the rewards of land (for instance) dangerous is the selling, and the implicit disrespect or denial of someone else's rights or claims to it. The commodities listed seem to be the ones whose sale is most likely to involve some perceived unfairness or injustice. Nor, probably, is the list complete, but these were the only transactions yielding bitter money of which I have been able, in a brief time, to learn; and as discussed later, there are many other transactions that are forbidden in various ways but do not produce bitter money.

We deal now first with land, tobacco, cannabis, and gold in turn. As it happens, each of these commodities has been associated with major social, economic, or political changes in the South Nyanza district of Luoland, where most of my interviews were conducted.[6] Roosters, considered last, are special in that their individual economic value is small but their symbolic associations strong.

Land

A profound and wide-ranging change in 20th-century Luoland has been the growth of a market in land, a process lately stimulated by the Kenya government's nationwide program of registering all farmland as private, individual property.

Like agrarian peoples all over eastern Africa, the Luo had no strictly private ownership (or, for that matter, communal ownership) in land as Europeans understand it before the arrival of Europeans in the late 19th century. Rather, Luo land rights depended on a complex interaction of principles that can only be sketched in roughest outline here.[7] Individuals and families acquired land use rights by virtue of real or putative membership in patrilineages or patriclans, by long residence in the territory of these groups or their larger federations (*ogendni*), or by territorial encroachments or conquest. Over the long term one could maintain cultivation rights to a particular piece of land by investing labor: in this respect, the Luo case was characteristic of land right systems all over the continent.[8] The system oscillated seasonally between individualistic and collectivistic principles, never reaching extremes: land to which an individual or family held fairly exclusive rights during the growing season became open grazing ground for neighbors after harvest. At any time, many different people and groups could have rights of different orders in a particular piece of land; and the rights of use, administration, and disposal were often held by different people. Land was not normally salable until well into the colonial period, though relatives could swap holdings or, where lineage elders agreed, invite outsiders onto lineage lands. Though women did not normally inherit land, when married they held well-recognized rights in the lands of their conjugal families, holding these in trust for their own unmarried sons.[9]

Territorial confinement of ethnic groups under colonial authority, the advent of the ox-plow, and the falling death rate due to medicine and consequent rises in population growth all contributed to competition for land and to local imbalances in the ratio of population to land in the first three decades of the 20th century. In Luoland the competition led to some strengthening of individual claims in places. But there were already strong sanctions against land sales. Toward the end of the 19th century, for instance, the last *jabilo* (diviner for the *oganda*) of Kanyamkago is said to have placed a curse on the selling of land there—a sign that at least someone was trying to sell. Kanyamkago residents now hold that his curse has killed neighbors who have sold their land—nearly everyone can think of examples—and that even the cattle of those guilty have died off. (Such curses are known elsewhere in East Africa.)[10] In the early 20th century, overt or covert land sales became a more familiar idea if not yet a common practice.[11]

Now they are becoming common practice. This was a part of the original design behind the registration of all farmland as private property. Set in motion by the British colonial government in 1954 as the continent's first nationwide attempt to "individualize" land, the processes of land consolidation, adjudication, and registration have continued under the national government since independence in 1963. Those who have studied the tenure reform in Luoland agree on several things. The registration has been a hard process for the government and for rural people, has endangered or diminished the legal land rights of women and other categories of persons, has failed to achieve its planned goals (except for a probable concentration of holdings, an explicit aim of the original plan), and is producing a land register that is quickly becoming obsolete.[12]

The Luo stiffly resisted the process until after Kenya's independence in 1963. They resisted for many reasons, some concerning preservation of their social structure and process. It is well known to East Africanists that the Luo conceive of land as a permanent lineage asset, closely linked with genealogical position, and as something not to let go lightly. Luo assess and defend claims to land by reference to ancestral graves: the dead are buried in the homestead, and the spirits remain around there when the homestead is eventually abandoned.

All in Luoland agree that the ancestors disapproved of land sales, and many Luo still do today. In explaining why, an elderly Kanyamkago woman told me cryptically that the land is (like) a magician *(lowo jajwok)*, adding that

> When we are born, we find it there; all that we eat comes from it; what we excrete goes back to it, and when we die we return to it. It feeds us and it swallows us.[13]

In a sense, selling land is selling the ancestors, and thus one's patrilineal kin; for these are so closely identified as to be in some respects the same.[14] The rewards that come from one come from the others too.

Luo say that ancestral spirits follow money obtained in land sales and ensure that it comes to no good for the seller. This money is *makech*, bitter. Luo believe that if a man sells land and buys livestock with it, either directly or indirectly, the animals or their offspring will die off by disease or other misfortune. If he first uses the animals in a bridewealth payment, the bride will die before long. According to one informant, this is because the bride, coming into the patrilineage, will eat the food from the land that has been cast out of the lineage. Seemingly everyone in Kanyamkago knows someone whose patriline has been ruined by the use of bitter money in bridewealth. A middle-aged man told his own story. In 1954, he said, he had harvested some tobacco, sold it, and bought a goat with the money. His goats multiplied, and he exchanged these for cattle, which he used in bridewealth payments for his sons' marriages. Now the sons wanted to have families of their own, but because of the bitter money, he doubted whether they and their wives would be able to produce healthy offspring.

Whether land sales will lead to ruin even today is a subject of much debate in Luoland. Many say they are waiting to see. One of my eldest women informants sighed that since the blacks had taken over from the whites in Kenya, everything had turned upside down, and perhaps now it was possible to get rich by selling land.[15]

Tobacco

Money from tobacco resembles money from land, in that it involves the spirits of ancestors, and it is partly these associations with ancestors that appear to make it "bitter." Tobacco also resembles land in that it has been the subject of an ambitious recent campaign from outside Luoland to push Luo agriculture into a market economy.

The Luo have known tobacco *(Nicotiana tabacum;* in Luo, *ndawa)* for generations, possibly since shortly after its introduction on the continent in the 16th century.[16]

Smoked mainly by elders until recent years, tobacco was grown in small quantities in the abandoned homes of dead relatives, where manure from the old cattle enclosures had made the soil especially fertile.[17] In Luoland the abandoned homestead enclosures are also the sites of ancestral graves. It was perhaps for this reason, combined with the fascination of fire and smoke, and the sometimes narcotic and even hallucinogenic effects of nicotine (see Schweinfurth 1878, vol. I:254), that the Luo thought of tobacco as a crop of the spirits of the dead.

The Luo have believed, and many still do today, that the spirits watched over the growing tobacco plants and followed the crop after harvest. Elders of both sexes smoked as a way of contacting spirits in times of trouble. They found smoking gave them extraordinary powers of memory: ancestors from the distant past with whom the smoker was not acquainted would appear to him or her, just as they could during a sleeping dream. Informants say the ancestors often appeared smoking pipes themselves. Evoking spirits by smoking was something of a gamble: the smoker had no choice of what spirit might appear, and the appearance of an unwelcome one could drive him or her insane. It was the spirits, too, who caused tobacco addiction and urged an elder to plant more of the crop.

Smoke appears to constitute its own conceptual category for the Luo. It is as much like a liquid as it is like air. The usual term for "to smoke" is *madho ndawa*, literally, to drink tobacco. Smoke is thought to wash away problems as water washes away dirt; and it could do so for a smoker just as for participants in special ritual sacrifices where meat was cooked. Elders will also say *ndawa mach*, tobacco is fire. So it is a product of the earth that may be associated with air, water, and fire at the same time. Tobacco connects elements of the ordinary world, and it connects the ordinary world with the spirit world. This last is a theme common to other Nilotic peoples too.[18]

Luo believe the spirits follow transactions where tobacco is involved and render unproductive wealth acquired through it. Like money from land sales, money from tobacco is *makech*, and it has to be kept strictly separate from lineage stock or bridewealth. If a man exchanges tobacco for livestock, either directly or indirectly, and uses the animals in a bridewealth payment, the bride will perish in fire and smoke, since she will have been procured through fire and smoke. Not even the animals' calves will do.[19] Selling tobacco involves the spirits in profane commerce, and this action taints wealth. It affects not only money, but also animal and human wealth.

There are other trepidations, too, surrounding tobacco. Of the countless Catholic and Protestant churches that together claim as

members most of the Luo today, nearly all have objections, strong or
mild, to tobacco production or use.[20] Among these are sects opposed
to tobacco in their European mother churches (e.g., the popular Seventh-Day Adventist Church), others whose African missions have imposed new strictures not found in the European mother churches (notably Anglican and Catholic churches), and a vast number of independent African Christian churches. Though smoking is nowhere explic-
itly condemned in the Judeo-Christian Bible, many Luo find passages
there to support its condemnation, such as Mark 7:21: "That which
proceedeth from the man, that defileth the man"—in this case, smoke
from the smoker's mouth. During the colonial period many converted
Luo decided tobacco was not just an ancestral spirits' crop, but Satan's
crop; others decided it was both. The new beliefs overlaid the old but
by no means expunged them. Tobacco was cursed, and most still seem
to think it is today.

But none of this has prevented the recent spread of tobacco as a
cash crop. In the late 1960s the British-American Tobacco Company
(BAT), the largest tobacco company in the Western world, had established its buying centers at Oyani and Taranganya, in South Nyanza.[21]
By 1982, BAT had contracted over 4000 farmers in Luo locations of
South Nyanza to build tobacco drying barns and to grow Virginia flue-
cured and other types of tobacco on parts of their own landholdings.

Tobacco has proved an extremely lucrative crop for smallholders.[22] They have made more money per hectare with tobacco than with
any other seasonal crop they grow.[23] But the inequalities in the distribution of the profits among local growers are enormous.[24] Men are
contracted and paid in cash as individuals, though they use mainly
family labor. The burden of the longer and duller tasks, especially
weeding, has been shifting to women. The scheme appears to be concentrating family wealth into male hands.[25] It is also undermining the
authority of elders, since BAT prefers younger men because of their
supposed energy, and since now, for the first time, junior men can
become richer than their fathers while staying at home. Tobacco has
called for adjustments in patterns of labor recruitment. Some men are
hiring help on a cash basis for the first time, for the day-and-night
chore of feeding wood into the curing barns in drying time. Others are
adapting old Luo forms of exchange labor, notably the *rika* (a small
circle of neighbors who work for each other in rotation). Though tobacco has brought about visible improvements in housing in Kanyamkago, many of the farmers are spending a large part of their tobacco
earnings on town drinking, prostitution, and other entertainments of
which their relatives disapprove. The spread of the tobacco crop in an
area where fundamentalist Christian churches predominate has ne-

cessitated adjustments in religious belief and practice.[26] While a few of the churches have remained dead set against tobacco growing, most have found rather clever ways to reconcile themselves with it.[27] In several, members who grow tobacco protect themselves by giving their local clergy a portion of their tobacco profits—call it a tithe or otherwise, the pattern is familiar from other walks of life—and the clergy arrange the rest with the spiritual or ecclesiastical powers, as need be.

Is tobacco money still bitter? Do the ancestral spirits and Christian demons still follow tobacco and the wealth that comes from it, now that the crop is big business? Some think not, and I have heard the reason given that the new tobacco is not grown just at abandoned homestead sites and therefore lacks some of the spiritual charges. But many Luo think old and new tobacco are bitter alike. Some will point to the frequent barn fires, others to floods and hailstorms. *"Piny oketh-ore,"* some elders will say, "the country is being spoiled."[28] Older women warn that tobacco wealth will not last, and will not help anyone's lineage, and many will tell of marriages and families that collapsed when tobacco money worked its way into bridewealth. It is widely claimed that money earned by growing tobacco gets spent faster than other money. Many farmers believe this is because the money is bitter and followed by spirits.[29] But others say they are unsure whether the new BAT tobacco yields bitter money, like the old local tobacco. As in the case of newly registered land, many say they have not had time to watch the effects on families and lineages: they are waiting to see.

To be on the safe side, farmers say, it is good to use tobacco money on food and clothes, or iron roofs—things not expected to last forever anyway. They say, do not use it to buy cattle or pay bridewealth; use maize money for that. But there seems to be a disjunction here between the real and the ideal. For when tobacco growers were questioned on how they had used their tobacco earnings in the previous year, livestock purchases were the most common response. A likely reason is that men, being the first to receive the tobacco earnings, are seeking to preserve part of the wealth as unchallengeable male property by converting it to livestock. But by converting bitter money into lineage property, they are risking the wrath of the spirits and of God. Some who have obtained livestock through tobacco earnings, and want to use it for bridewealth, are trying to "launder" the wealth by selling the stock, buying other animals with the proceeds, and using them instead. Conservatives say this will never work.

Cannabis

Cannabis sativa (marijuana, called *njaga* in Luo and *bhang* in many East African languages) is another crop that Luo elders grew and smoked in the past. They planted it where tobacco grew, in the abandoned homestead sites, and Luo men smoked it to communicate with the ancestors, among other purposes. The ancestral spirits were thought to protect cannabis gardens, as they protected tobacco gardens. At the same time, however, a small amount of cannabis kept inside a house was believed to ward away malevolent spirits and to protect a family from cholera, believed to be a spirit-borne disease. Cannabis was a medicine, then, associated with ancestors in both positive and negative ways.

Cannabis smoking, like tobacco smoking, has now spread to juniors and cannabis has become a common commodity in the informal economy of both city and countryside in Kenya. Cannabis is forbidden both by national law and by Kenyan Christian churches—frequent condemnations appear in Kenyan newspapers—but the commerce, particularly among young men with buyers in the towns, is lively. Once planted, cannabis can grow and reproduce quickly and with little labor input. "It's like stealing," stated a Luo man. This seems to be another reason why money or other goods obtained through cannabis are bitter.

Gold

Another economic and social change of the 20th century has been the use of Luo land and labor from the 1930s onward for foreign-owned gold mines, including Macalder's Mine, a small British-owned gold mine in the western part of the location, 15 kilometers from Lake Victoria and the same distance from the Tanzanian border.[30] Though the "Native Reserves" had been protected by the Native Trust Lands Ordinance of 1930, mineral rights still belonged to the British Crown and a new Mining Ordinance was passed in 1931 that effectively allowed the Provincial Commissioner to issue prospecting permits to settlers on payment of a 20 shilling fee and a £25 deposit (Fearn 1961:128–129; Hay 1972:221). Small prospectors flowed into the province, followed by agents of larger, London-registered companies. These companies acquired land rights on leasehold. Their invasions of local farm and homestead lands were compensated by commuted rent, in cash. This was unacceptable to the Nyanza Africans, whose

land transactions had customarily been redeemable at will by the original owner. It was particularly unacceptable to those who had learned
of the supposed "protection" under the 1930 ordinance (Fearn
1961:143–146; cf. Hay 1972:221). Five thousand and eighty-one Luo
and as many Luhya, mostly men, were at work in the Nyanza mines
by 1935. In that year, the peak year of the industry, the Africans
worked for an average of £6 a year (Fearn 1961:130). This was not a bad
wage by the standards of other opportunities Africans had (Hay
1972:222–223). But the European staff members earned 39 times as
much per capita (calculated from Fearn 1961:130). Cash wages paid to
Africans attracted new Indian and other Asian traders, with new commodities. Most of the gold was exported from Kenya as bullion. So
while the gold rush brought some welcome new jobs and commerce
to the region, it also meant land dispossessions, a gender differential
in earning power, discriminatory licensing, locally unprecedented
wage inequalities, and ultimate extraction of the precious metal for
parts unknown.

The Second World War and its equipment shortages brought
problems to the European mining firms from which they never re-
covered, and they abandoned the Nyanza mines by the early 1950s.
Although Macalder's is still officially defunct, some local farmers still
mine the shafts and surrounding fields, illegally, on a small scale.[31] A
few also pan for gold in local streams. Local traders serve as middlemen in a covert trade linking these small prospectors to Nairobi gold
buyers.

As with the other commodities, Kanyamkago informants will tell
of neighbors whose families have suffered grave misfortunes after selling gold to buy livestock. (This is not, of course, the kind of story that
anyone is likely to tell about him or herself.) An elderly woman in Kanyamkago told of her husband's brother, Dalmas Nyayal, who, when
young in the 1930s, had found gold on a visit to Kihancha, part of the
Kuria country.[32] He used the gold to buy cows and distributed these
to the eldest three of his four brothers. They used the cows for their
bridewealth, but he did not. The brothers all died, and so did all their
wives but one. But, at the time of fieldwork, Dalmas Nyayal was still
alive and living with his three wives and their children—to the informant, the picture of a successful man.

In another rumored instance, Okello Okwach of Karachuonyo,
South Nyanza, is said to have sold a substantial amount of gold, and
used the proceeds to buy 80 head of cattle, which he used to marry
two more wives. He also used some to educate his son to secondary
level, enabling the son to find work later as a headmaster in several
successive primary schools. But very gradually Okello Okwach's cattle

all died off, forcing him away to seek work in some of the towns. The son went to search for him, found him, and persuaded him to return home. Okwach is said to have turned foul-tempered toward his wives and other members of the family. He began beating the wives and coercing them into sexual acts at strange times. The son and the son's mother conspired to murder him, and they cut his body to pieces. Nor was peace restored even then: the family continued to decline and was reported almost gone by the time of the telling.

Some informants say that money from gold sales is bitter because it is a product of the land that is obtained with very little work, in relation to its value. Unlike money from, say, sorghum or maize, bitter money has involved too little sweat *(luya)*. Gold sales are illegal except with a license, virtually impossible for a Luo smallholder to obtain, but elders today say gold rewards were *makech* even before it became illegal. There are women working independently or grinding, panning, and washing what their male relatives dig up, but it seems the rewards have most often gone directly into men's hands.

Roosters

Beliefs about bitter money are full of metaphors. Just as the bride procured through tobacco sales can be expected to die in fire and smoke, Luo remember their elders' saying in the past that a bride obtained through the sale or barter of roosters for cattle would fly about like a hen, in adultery. Roosters remain among the objects of sales taboos; they still yield bitter blessings.

Why roosters are included, in Luo minds, must be explained in terms of their symbolism, since the individual economic value of the birds is small. Luo consider a home incomplete without a rooster. Like the sharpened pole sticking straight up from a thatch rooftop in a homestead with a living male head, the rooster stands for maleness. A Luo term for rooster, *thwon,* also means male or hero, rather as the English term "cock" has referred for centuries to the male organ as well as the animal. The rooster's polygamy is associated with human polygyny, a man's route to prestige and, in the past at least, often to wealth. It stands for sexual potency.

The rooster carries other related meanings. It is conceptually linked with the continuity of the lineage, and with the progress of civilization into the wilderness. In the Luo *buru* ceremony, which commemorates a man's death some time after the funeral, a rooster is taken from his homestead and cooked and eaten in the *thim* or bush. Among other things, this is thought to mark the end of his homestead as well as of the man's life. When a young married man and his wife found a new homestead, the man ritually receives a rooster and an axe from his father's. In the past, Luo say, it was variously customary to take fire, a spear, a shield, and a euphorbia plant (used for enclosing the homestead) too. Now these things are no longer taken along, but significantly, the rooster still is: it is considered absolutely essential. The homestead rooster is a special one. Its health is associated with the well-being of the family.[33] A bird with a floppy crest is a bad sign; this should stand up tall. When the rooster grows old and weak, a man cooks it and consumes it ritually with elders, to ensure the family does not decline with it, and thereafter he regards a young offspring rooster as the living symbol of his family.[34]

The rooster is not a peculiarly Luo symbol; it is important to other Kenyan ethnic groups and has been adopted as a national symbol as well. The rooster appears brandishing an axe (inside a shield, between lions rampant, with crossed spears—all associated with wilderness) in the center of the emblem of the Kenya African National Union, now the sole legitimate political party in the nation. The emblem is emblazoned on the reverse of all coins. The rooster was sometimes associated with the late President Jomo Kenyatta, and Jogoo House (*jogoo* is Swahili for rooster) in Nairobi remains the office of the Vice President.

To sell the homestead rooster, among the Luo at least, is to sell one's masculinity and authority, and to betray one's home and patriline. This powerful, polysemic symbol means too much to be converted freely to 20 shillings.

Some Questions Remaining

There are questions on which Luo feel uncertain or divided in opinions. Every belief system contains some uncertainties and logical inconsistencies, and it is these that give a system its flexibility for adaptation to novel circumstances and new questions. It is these, too, that allow the beliefs to survive occasions of conflicting evidence. Some of these questions, however, would merit further research.

Is bitterness an absolute quality or one existing in degrees? Some speak of it rather as an absolute—as if nothing could be just slightly bitter—but at the same time, Luo seem to worry more about large amounts of bitter money than small amounts.

Can barter of a forbidden commodity have the same adverse effects, and in the same degree, as a sale? Some say yes, but the use of money seems to heighten the dangers. Whereas money received as a "windfall" is unambiguously bitter, if a material good is received this way and sold for money, some say this money will not be bitter. In some sense it is "prelaundered" through the material exchange. Rewards first obtained in cash are the most dangerous; the currency is the salient element. Yet this belief does not diminish many informants' certainty that commodities like land, gold, or tobacco produce dangerous, bitter money from the start, and that this cannot be laundered into clean money by a series of exchanges.

Most reports about bitter money emphasize consequences to the seller who obtains the money—let the seller beware. On whether a buyer may suffer too, opinions seem to differ locally. In using bitter money Luo worry most about marriage, but funerals are other sacred activities from which bitter money should probably be kept out. For what other purposes must one not use it? Like other people, Luo acknowledge their spiritual world as not wholly predictable.

How widely are beliefs about bitter money held, and how old are they? Beliefs about bitter money are held throughout Luoland. Though I have found no written records specifically about these beliefs, or of similar ones elsewhere in the Lake Victoria region, Luhya informants have reported there are some similar beliefs in their home country in Western Province, just north of the Luo country. It would be surprising if no other peoples in the region drew similar distinctions between good and evil money. No one interviewed claimed to know how old the sales taboos are, but the taboo on land sales in Kanyamkago appears to date from at least the last decades of the 19th century, and here, at least, there is some documentation.[35] Informants insisted that the tobacco sales taboo is much older than the BAT buying station in Kanyamkago: some claim it existed before the establishment of fundamentalist Christian church missions and independent Christian churches in the area.[36] It seems likely that a concept of "bitter money" or some similar idea has existed for generations, but that the specific commodities or transactions associated with it have changed over time and space as some transactions have become more common and as the Luo have perceived them as dangerous to the fabric of society.[37]

Who formulates the ideas to begin with is, of course, equally hard to tell. No "Académie Française" seeks to control Luo custom centrally. It seems a few unusually perceptive or imaginative people build upon more commonly held sentiments, and, as in epic myth, chains of tellers make adjustments, adding bits of their own knowledge or wisdom while passing the word along. It may be, too, that some of today's "traditions" are being projected into the past.

Belief in bitter money is very much alive today. For many it is science—there is evidence all around to support it, and little to contradict it. It is most often elders who believe today in bitter money, as one might expect; juniors tend to be more skeptical or unsure on the subject, and usually turn to elders when wanting to know more. But the age division is far from clear: a few of all ages will profess to reject the entire notion, and perhaps some will grow to accept it later in life, even as formal schooling and Christianity lead others to reject it. The fluidity with which Luo mix elements of their local beliefs with elements of Christianity from various churches suggests that the idea may be adapted to new circumstances for some time to come.

The Ritual Purification of Money and Its Holders

Bitter money is convertible to good money, which will "stick" to its owner's homestead, by a purification ceremony (*oso*) led by a ritual specialist (*ajuoge*, sing. *ajuoga*).[38] A purification ritual for bitter money can be a rather frightening thing because of the unknown forces invoked, and it is performed only where a large amount of money is concerned: some considered 10,000 to 20,000 shillings as a minimum, but there is no clear cutoff.[39] Nor is a ceremony performed for just *any* bitter money. The ceremonies are more common for gold than for tobacco. This may be because gold is considered in a sense to be money already when it reaches one's hands, whereas tobacco is not. Purification ceremonies appear to be most common during the rainy seasons, when anxieties about damages to forthcoming harvests are highest. Most think a purification rite should be conducted soon after the money is brought home: the day after, ideally, or as soon thereafter as a ritual specialist can be engaged and provisions procured. As it happens, however, unrelated *ajuoge* living far from one's home are often preferred. They are considered not only to have greater power than those who are neighbors or kin, but also to be more discreet, being less entangled in local social life, and less jealous of the new wealth.[40]

No great rewards in Luo life are obtained without spiritual intervention, and an ostensible aim of a purification ceremony is to thank the spirit or spirits that provided the bitter money. If this is not done, they will ensure the money comes to no good. Most often, the spirit is assumed to be one in the male line. A son might let his father arrange the ritual, and a male homestead head may have it performed on behalf of his homestead.

Descriptions of the ceremonies vary.[41] Informants asked about standard practice sometimes begin by describing an "ideal" ceremony, with a large crowd assembled and the sacrifice of a bull, and end up talking about something much more modest, apparently more in line with present convention at least. All members of the lineage (in this context, *anyuola*) must come, some informants claim—but in a segmentary system, this must of course depend on how one defines the lineage, as well as on how seriously the ideal is taken. Recently, it seems to have been more common for the owner of the bitter money to hold a smaller meal with a few guests from the neighborhood who may or may not be kin.[42]

An ideal purification rite must involve blood sacrifice. The animal should be male: a bull (which must have horns), a ram, or other; but a female may be used on occasion.[43] The *ajuoga*, who may have come the night before the ceremony, may witness the slaughter in the morning, but it may be done by anyone. The sacrificer slices the animal's throat with a knife. Members of the homestead roast the meat, including the intestines, over fire, and all present eat of it. Beer is drunk (traditionally grain beer, with long straws from a single pot) and may contribute to singing; some also mention food including sesame gruel, cow's butter, and fish. The meal should be eaten in the center of the homestead.

In most versions, in Kanyamkago at least, the *ajuoga* openly prepares a mixture of water and herbal medicines (together called *manyasi*) together with chyme from the animal's stomach, in a small calabash. The possessor of the bitter money sips it, and the *ajuoga* sprinkles it onto the money (or the gold, in one report), and around the homestead, inside and outside the house or houses, and on animals of the homestead. He pours it on the adults of the homestead, but not on children, since they are assumed unable to make money. The possessor of the bitter wealth is expected to explain to the gathering how he obtained it.[44] The *ajuoga* may add herbal medicines to the food and conduct prayers. The blood of the sacrificed animal, the smoke of the fire, and the remnants of meat left around and outside the homestead are all thought to reach the ancestors; the blood and meat feed them. The flowing blood and the smoke are also thought to wash away evil. Some also say the departing guests take the spirits away with them.

Luo Christians commonly claim not to conduct such purification rites, at least not with animal sacrifices; but some are said to convene religious gatherings in their houses, with sermons, prayers, meals, and drink, in order to bless bitter money.[45] In these meetings they may drink tea, or as one informant told me rather to my surprise, even bottled soft drinks.

If the details of a purification rite are not attended to properly, it is said, it may do more harm than good. Some try to conduct the rites after spending the money, but this sequence is frowned upon. Informants told me of acquaintances who had died or gone insane because the wrong herbs had been used; one contrasted three of these with a man whose ritual had been well conducted and who had grown very rich: "ten wives or more."

Oso is more than a purification of money itself. It is a rite of passage for the transgressor of a norm—the one who has received the "bitter blessing"—and his family.[46] Selling land, tobacco, gold, cannabis, or the homestead rooster is rather like selling one's mother or father, and in a sense it *is* selling them; it is a gravely antisocial act.[47] Not just the money earned, but also the seller and those in close contact, become *makech*. If bitter money continues to circulate from one holder to another, the danger is not thought to circulate with it, but sticks with the one who committed the evil act and with his family. The purification ritual makes him or her fit to act as a member of society again. Bitterness is not just an attribute of money: it is an attribute of people.

Notes

1. The findings about bitter money sketched here were made toward the end of (and incidentally to) a field research project on rural land rights and credit systems, between 1980 and 1983. Since only a short time could be devoted in the field to bitter money beliefs, their variations over time and space are not yet known. Most of the information on bitter money here comes from Kanyamkago Location, South Nyanza District, but bitter money from forbidden transactions is a familiar idea throughout Luoland at least, and widely associated with the commodities discussed here.

2. The root in DhoLuo is *kech; ma* is an adjectival prefix. The term conflates various meanings of evil or harm; in noun form *kech* also means hunger or famine. Though many Luo speak of money's "bitterness" with the explicit simile of taste in the mouth, there seems to be no opposite like "sweet" money; instead, money that is not *makech* is simply *pesa maber*, "good money." The evil state is thus marked, while the opposite is unmarked.

3. Once "dirty money" is in our possession, we may feel little compunction about the uses to which we can put it. To North American academics, the origin of grant money does not normally restrict its usability. Fulbright awards come from American arms sales abroad, Rhodes scholarships from gruesome racial exploitation in southern African mines, Nobel prizes from high explosives. Academic scholarships are a favorite way for weapon mongers to launder "dirty money" back into respectability, a kind of atonement. Scholars seem to use these funds with more pride than shame, reasoning sometimes that the real dirty work was done by someone else, and that taking is different from contributing. But where the initial earner of "dirty" money also spends it on other ethically dubious purposes, public opprobrium can be great. The American press deemed the "Iran-Contra" scandal of the Reagan administra-

tion in the United States worse than the sum of two separate scandals in different parts of the world, because the funds earned in one covert illegal military activity were used in another, allegedly by some of the same people.

4. Ocholla-Ayayo (1976:241) lists the Luo proverb, *Kik icham gima Jamichiere onego, kata chiemo mokwal*, "Do not eat stolen food, especially meat of stolen livestock." It can make one ill at least: in a way more literal than in the proverb, one man's meat *is* another man's poison. Compare the Kikuyu proverbs, *Indo ciene iri mutino*, "Stolen things bring in misfortune," and *Mũgũĩ utarĩ wa awa nĩ ũkũndembũrĩra thiaka*, "The arrow which is not my father's pierces my quiver," meaning roughly the same (Barra 1987:26, 55).

5. The "spirit of the gift," reported by Robert Hertz among the Maori and made famous by Marcel Mauss, is what compels a gift recipient to reciprocate or pass the gift along, and thus to be a member of society. Mauss writes of the now famous Maori *hau*,

> Even when abandoned by the giver, it still forms a part of him. . . . To keep this thing is dangerous, not only because it is illicit to do so, but also because it comes morally, physically, and spiritually from a person. Whatever it is, food, possessions, women, children or ritual, it retains a magical and religious hold over the recipient. The thing given is not inert. It is alive and often personified, and strives to bring to its original clan and homeland some equivalent to take its place. [Mauss 1967 [1925]:8–10]

Much of this comes close to the Luo conception of bitter money, except that the giving and taking may be reversed.

6. In fieldwork I learned that several commodities produced bitter money, and saw only after learning this that the commodities tended to be associated with major changes I had been observing in Luo society.

7. See Shipton (1984a, 1984b), and sources cited there specifically on the preregistration systems of tenure in Luoland; Okoth-Ogendo (1976, 1978) discusses Kenyan tenure systems more generally from a sociolegal perspective. A monograph I am now preparing compares the Luo experience of land privatization with those of other African agrarian peoples.

8. The best general survey of African systems of land tenure with reference to the principle that "work creates rights" remains Meek (1946). (It also contains useful chapters on other parts of the then British empire.) The idea that the investment of labor is what creates property relations between people and things (or between people in respect of things) is an old idea, however; it was the central point of John Locke's "labor theory of value" in the *Second Treatise of Government*.

9. The listed works of Pala (1977, 1980) and Hay (1972, 1982) discuss the preregistration land rights of Luo women in some detail.

10. Compare this finding of Moore's (1986:267) on the Chagga of Mt. Kilimanjaro, Tanzania:

> It is said even today that cursed land, lands wrongfully appropriated and then cursed by the rightful owner cannot be sold by the appropriator or his descen-

dants at any price if the story of the curse is known and believed. Thus there are supernatural reasons to have clear "title," that is, in this system, a clear right to sell land.

Farther afield, Bourdieu (1977:175) describes how the land of Kabylia "settles its scores" with farmers who have abused it.

11. See DeWilde 1967:130–131; Dundas 1913:55; Fearn 1961:34; and the notes of the Kenya Land Commission (1934:2294, 2299).

12. See Coldham (1978, 1979), Okoth-Ogendo (1976, 1978), Pala (1977, 1983), and Shipton (1988) on the registration process and its effects there. These sources also cite other reports based on first-hand observations in Luoland. See also Glazier (1985) and Haugerud (1983) on Embu District.

13. The phrase *chamo lowo*, to eat (from) land, can also mean to inherit it.

14. See Gudeman (1986:40–41) for a discussion of the continuum from "as if" to "as being" models. The ontological problems implied in "as being" models are old, however, and much debated since Evans-Pritchard's famous reports (1956) that to the Nuer, "twins are birds" and sacrificed cucumbers "are" bulls.

15. Of course, not all shared her political views!

16. The crop had spread quickly through the continent upon its introduction (Akehurst 1981; Brooks 1937, vol. I:41–42). Luo call local strains of tobacco *ndap nyaluo*, "Luo tobacco," suggesting how well the crop had become incorporated into Luo life before the start of the BAT project. Until colonial times, Luo elders smoked tobacco in fairly short-stemmed pipes made of clay, Kisii soapstone, or goatskin; but over the past few decades home-rolled and mass-produced cigarettes have almost completely taken over. Pipe stems and bowls had male and female sexual associations, respectively. Today, men smoke cigarettes with the burning end outward, but women commonly smoke them with the burning end inside the mouth. (According to some, women first began doing this in the evenings to avoid the notice of missionaries who disapproved of their smoking. A second reason is that the tobacco burns more slowly and delivers more nicotine. Another obvious Freudian explanation suggests itself, as with the pipe parts.)

17. Some elders say that in precolonial times the Luo harvested tobacco where elephants had defecated.

18. Johnson (1980:216) mentions that elder Suba (Luo speakers of Bantu descent living near Kanyamkago in South Nyanza) use tobacco in purification ceremonies for accidental killers, though its significance there is unclear. R. G. Abrahams (personal communication) has observed that among the Labwor, a Lwoo-speaking Ugandan group related to the Kenya Luo, tobacco is an especially potent article used in interpersonal blessings (pressed against the forehead, inserted between toes and into armpits, and held in hand). His unpublished field notes read, "It seems its [the blessing's] strength is connected with kec-ness [like Luo *kech*-ness] of tobacco. Other aspects of this are that a person who steals tobacco will die very quickly if its owner curses him and there is also some belief that a person who has very, very much tobacco in his house will be killed by it." Evans-Pritchard (1956:221) has noted that "In vio-

lent storms Nuer, fearful of the lightning, throw small pieces of tobacco into the air, asking God to take them, and saying that they have paid him ransom with this offering." Lienhardt observed on the Nuer and Dinka shrines of their deity Deng Dit, "No man can safely approach it without making some small offering, usually by throwing tobacco in the direction of the shrine" (1961:101; see also pp. 153–154, 259 on tobacco offerings to divinity, clan divinities, and ancestral ghosts).

19. Tobacco taboos also apply to women's out-marriages as well as to in-marriages. A bridegroom must not take tobacco to the home of his bride—as one elderly widow put it, she would then have to make up some excuse not to marry him, like "he's not beautiful enough," or "he's not wealthy enough." Nor must her family give any to him, or sell any for food or livestock to be given to him, or the marriage will be spoiled.

20. But packaged cigarettes and home-rolled tobacco are now ubiquitous commodities in Luoland, and despite the disapproval of many of the Euro-American and independent churches, many men and women of all ages smoke.

21. The occasion was the nationalization of its Tanzanian tobacco operations, which until then had supplied tobacco to Kenya.

22. This paragraph is a cursory summary of findings presented in more detail in Shipton (1985:288–309); see also Acland (1980).

23. Except perhaps cannabis; records on this are lacking. By growing tobacco, in the early 1980s in Kanyamkago Location, Luo could normally make profits per hectare about 2.8 times those possible by growing hybrid maize with all recommended inputs (which few actually applied); or about 4.6 times as much as by growing cotton. The average South Nyanza tobacco grower's net profit of 3400 shillings from a half-hectare in the crop was enough to buy four bulls or cows, or 1.1 hectares of good farm land. Alternatively, it would pay secondary school fees for 1.6 children for a year, or almost finance an iron roof for an average-sized Luo house. In the BAT pricing policy, quality could be multiplied by quantity, permitting occasional net profits of over 30,000 shillings per hectare (about $3000): a truly extraordinary profit by Luo agricultural standards. See Shipton 1985: chapt. 13.

24. In 1982, for instance, the highest-earning quartile of 128 registered BAT tobacco growers in a sublocation of Kanyamkago earned 68% of the total tobacco earnings, while the lowest-earning quartile earned only 1% (compiled from BAT records). One reason for the poor distribution of the rewards is that tobacco is graded on a wide scale according to quality, and therefore quality can be multiplied by quantity for the best growers.

25. As of 1982, 96% of the 128 registered tobacco growers in the Kanyamkago sublocation studies were male.

26. Long's study of the Lala of Zambia (1968:242) found that Jehovah's Witnesses were often the first to adopt a new commercial Turkish tobacco crop. His explanation, inspired by Weber (1930), focuses on what he perceives as their individualistic ethic.

27. In the early 1980s, the Gospels Church warned members who grow tobacco but did not expel them. The Roho Msanda Holy Ghost Church and

the Pentecostal Holiness Church had decided that their lay members may grow tobacco, but not their clergy. The Seventh-Day Adventist Church and the Legio Maria, two of the churches that most adamantly resisted tobacco growing in the early BAT years in South Nyanza, had later, after much debate, allowed their members to grow tobacco. But they stipulated that none who did so could take communion.

28. Compare the Bemba attribution of 1930s copper price collapses to the displeasure of the ancestors (Richards 1939:235; also discussed in Gudeman 1986:94). Findings like these are fairly common patterns in rural African studies.

29. In part of a survey I conducted, men and women of 107 households in Kanyamkago Location were asked whether farmers found this a problem, and if so, why it happened. (Possible answers were not prompted.) Thirty-eight percent responded that it was a problem because of the spirits of the dead; this was by far the most common answer. This is not, of course, the kind of question best answered by survey, and I believe the proportion of farmers who think the spirits cause the money to disappear quickly may be rather higher.

30. For historical reconstructions of the mining era, see Fearn (1961:123–150) and Hay (1972:218–224).

31. The Trading in Unwrought Precious Metals Act of 1933, revised 1984, states that "No person shall buy, sell, deal in, receive, or dispose of by way of barter, pledge or otherwise, either as principal or agent, any unwrought precious metal" without a license from the Commissioner of Mines and Geology or an agent (*Laws of Kenya*, Ch. 309, sect. 3).

32. In reports about incidents concerning bitter money, I have changed the personal names.

33. Far afield, Clifford Geertz's well-known article (1972) on the Balinese cockfight describes some other ways men can identify with roosters. More broadly, Eugenia Shanklin (1985) reviews anthropological literature on domestic animals and their symbolism; see pp. 392–396 on "animals as metaphors" for humans.

34. Compare some other eastern African peoples' historical customs of killing a leader weakening from age or illness to ensure that society does not weaken with him. Some variants have been found or indirectly reported among the Nilotic Dinka (Lienhardt 1961:298–319) and Shilluk (Evans-Pritchard 1963:76) of Sudan, distant cousins of the Luo; and the Bantu-speaking Nyoro of Uganda (Beattie 1971:105n) and Bemba of what is now Zambia (Richards 1940:98n).

35. See also the Kenya Land Commission 1934:2147, 2198, 2201, 2294; Wilson 1961:75–80 on the Luo; and Wagner 1956:77–78 on the Luhya.

36. Tobacco has been bought and sold, if only on a small scale, in and around Luoland for generations (Wagner 1956, vol. II:166–167).

37. While numerous written and oral reports suggest that sales of land have been considered incorrect behavior for several generations, there appears to be no available documentation of corresponding beliefs about sales of

tobacco, gold, or cannabis, except as concern national law. It is likely that gold became associated with bitterness during or after the 1930s, when mining became common in Nyanza, but this is only conjecture.

38. *Dolo, misango,* and *liswa* (which can all mean sacrifice) are other terms I have heard denoting purification rituals, and *dilo* is also reported.

39. In the early 1980s, the Kenya shilling was worth about 10 U.S. cents.

40. The preference for shamans, diviners, etc. living far away from one's home is a pattern observed in many other societies, in Africa south of the Sahara and elsewhere. Some may be considered more powerful precisely *because* their ordinary social roles are less familiar.

41. I have not had the opportunity to witness an *oso* ritual. In Hubert's and Mauss's classic schema emphasizing the distinction between sacred and profane in ritual and the difference between "sacralization" and "desacralization" (1964), the sacrifices the Luo describe would be "desacralization" in that they are attempts to free someone of tainting impurity. De Heusch analyzes African animal sacrifices, modifying Hubert's and Mauss's distinction (de Heusch 1985: chaps. 5–6, p. 213; see also Shanklin 1985:396–398 and sources cited therein). De Heusch also analyzes some apparent meanings of chyme in sacrificial rites of the Thonga in southern Africa (pp. 72–82); human contact with chyme is also important in Luo rituals of peacemaking, and of separation as in the establishment of new land boundaries. See also Abe's description (1978:10–11) of purification rituals (which he calls *dilo*) among Luo of Kamagambo Location, South Nyanza.

42. This diminution of ceremony through time, or because of practical constraints, is reminiscent of the famous Nuer sacrifices of cucumbers in lieu of bulls (Evans-Pritchard 1956:128). Of course, ritual gestures may also be exaggerated in oral lore, or concealed from foreigners suspected to be opposed.

43. No special color has been mentioned to me for these animals, but in other Luo sacrifices, red, black, or white animals are variously preferred, as in many other African societies south of the Sahara. There are many surface parallels between Luo sacrifices and those studied in more detail by Evans-Pritchard (1956) among the Nuer and Lienhardt (1961) among the Dinka: for instance, in the uses of chyme and medicinal solutions, and beliefs about blood and smoke.

44. For this reason, it is said, thieves are not likely to have purification ceremonies, though their wealth is bitter. But I have heard of rituals conducted such that their reason remains secret to the convener and *ajuoga.*

45. Nor, of course, should one overlook the similarities between "traditional" Luo blood sacrifices and Catholic communion rites.

46. See van Gennep 1960; Ocholla-Ayayo 1976:240–241; Turner 1969. Purification rites are performed upon many other transgressions of norms in Luo culture, for instance where one has committed murder, where land has been cursed, where a woman has refused to sleep with her husband, or where two women with breast-feeding children have fought.

47. Indeed, a Luo arguing against land alienations before the Kenya Land Commission in 1932 summed up his feelings by saying, "The land is our mother" (Kenya Land Commission 1934:2166).

5

Explaining Bitter Money: Strain and "Resistance Belief"

In an age of political economy theory focusing on links between local and supralocal levels of society, an obvious starting point for explaining bitter money is the nature of past interventions in Luo economy from outside. As Nash's (1979) and Taussig's (1980) analyses of devil's money in South America, discussed later, suggest, hard experience with foreign extractive systems can breed creative ideological response in conceptions of cash.

The commodities whose sale yields bitter money tend to have several things in common. First, they tend to be local commodities belonging to or produced by Luo, but sought now or in the past by Europeans. The gold mine and the tobacco scheme were foreign attempts to derive profits from the Luo land, using Luo labor. Tobacco, cannabis, and gold are all associated with land: they are products of particular places attached to particular descent groups, and thus to ancestors. Clearly, in some sense, sales of these objects are a betrayal, a capitulation to foreign pressures. Is bitter money a symbolic expression of resistance to foreign incursions?

Religious resistance is a familiar theme in and around Luoland. Most notable in 20th-century history has been the nativistic Mumbo movement, which sprang up in South Nyanza (including what is now Kisii) in about 1913 and lasted, or continued reappearing, for some forty years. British punitive military expeditions in Kisii unwittingly fed the cult resistance, but its apparent causes were multiple: they clearly included economic and political degradation, psychological stresses, and half-successful syncretisms between local religions and Christianity. Originating when, supposedly, a giant snake from Lake Victoria swallowed a Luo named Onyango and gave him commandments, Mumboism prophesied that the Europeans would soon leave Nyanza and a golden age of justice would begin. It called for the sacrifice of all livestock—to be replaced later by herds that would emerge from the lake—and it abjured all European customs (Wipper 1977:3).[1]

Among other things, the Mumboites prophesied that when the great day came, they would be able to smoke cannabis as much as they wished—in reality, Mumboites smoked it and were often harassed by colonial authorities for doing so. They said they would also be reunited with the dead.[2] That ancestors appeared as prominent elements of this resistance movement would seem, in a sense, to underscore their role in the current "bitter money" belief system as symbols of local autonomy. Animal sacrifices and the smoking of intoxicants are modes of transcendence for the living: at once ways of gaining access to the spirit world and of proclaiming solidarity with a popular protest cause.

The Mumbo cult and other spirit possession movements in Nyanza have resembled hundreds of other revitalization movements in Africa in their expression of grievance against colonial subjugation.[3] Mumboism was one of passive protest, not violent resistance.[4] Belief in bitter money can be interpreted as a quieter form of resistance still: it too combines the old and new religions, but it is a conceptual structure with no particular cult following.

There are other examples of "resistance beliefs," as I shall call them, in East Africa. One is the anti-European mythology of the Fipa in southwestern Tanzania. Roy Willis (1973:253–255) relates there the myth of the prophet "Kaswa," who decries the depersonalization of economic relations under European capitalism, and who deplores the treatment of land and plants under this system. Kaswa says,

> Something is coming, creeping, from the east—something with god-like powers [Europeans]. . . . O you people, you are going to be robbed of your country. . . . Everything becomes currency, *ifyuuma* [precolonial iron pieces used as currency]—grass and the very earth itself.

The prophet continues (in Willis's phrasing):

> In this alarmingly transformed world, the products of man's social labour take on a frightening life of their own, so that the motorcars of the Europeans, the "Monstrous inventors," have "protruding eyes" (head-lamps), while their anuses (exhaust pipes) exude fire. [Willis 1973:254]

This is more than protest politics or protest religion: in a sense, it is protest art. But rather than the creation of a mere individual, bitter money, the Mumbo myth, and the Kaswa tale are truly *popular* creations. As Comaroff has remarked about the religious movement called Zionism among the Tshidi people in South Africa,

We deal here with the culture of more than a millenarian minority; we confront the coherent response—the distinct order of value and practice—of a large sector of the population on the cultural and economic fringe. [1985:263]

Bitter money betrays a bitterness in attitudes of the Luo about their place in the world. A people who may once have thought themselves somehow central have been peripheralized: they have become involved in a world where the real centers of wealth, power, and influence seem to lie far away and out of reach. But in bitter money the Luo also express a pride in what they see as their beleaguered customs. In these reflections the Luo are far from unique in the peaceful corners of Africa.

Bitterness and Agricultural Capital: Why the "Resistance" Approach, though Useful, Is not Quite Enough to Explain Luo Bitter Money

How satisfactorily does the attractive answer of "resistance belief" explain bitter money? Does a history of foreign exploitation in a commodity necessarily make it bitter? There are two ways to see. One is to ask whether there are commodities associated with foreign exploitation that do not yield bitter money. The other is to ask whether there are other commodities that yield bitter money, but are not associated with foreign exploitation.

A test case, to start, is sugarcane. This crop has represented an even more important investment of foreign capital in rural Nyanza than tobacco. Like tobacco, sugar has been grown in the area for generations, but has recently become an object of keen international interest there. In the colonial period, Asian-owned sugar factories and plantations arose in what is now the Kisumu District of Luoland, where they still function. Since 1978, the South Nyanza (SONY) Sugar Company has run a World Bank-financed factory and nucleus plantation at Awendo, surrounded by smallholder contract farmers (or "outgrowers") extending in a circle 26 miles across, including a part of Kanyamkago that overlaps with the tobacco contract farming circle of BAT. The nucleus estate was established by the eviction of several thousand farming households. Using heavy machinery to prepare land and collect cane on both the nucleus estate and the surrounding smallholdings, and gangs of poorly housed laborers paid at subsistence wages for harvesting, SONY epitomizes much of the worst in capitalist agriculture. Its foreign-born managers, its tractor-drivers, and its cane weighers (always suspected of crooked dealings, rightly or wrongly) are unpopular with local farmers. Its extension agents, traveling in nearly empty Land Rovers, are considered arrogant and aloof. Its machinery has dramatically altered the landscape in ways likely to speed soil erosion. Payments from sugarcane, coming to a family less than once a year, are even larger than those for tobacco; and again, they come almost exclusively into male hands.

But despite all this, the Luo of the area do not, or at least did not by the early 1980s, classify money from sugarcane as bitter. It was simply ordinary money, "good" money. Similarly, money from coffee, grown in parts of the South Nyanza uplands, and from cotton, a crop grown in the lakeside lowlands since early in the century and closely associated with colonial exploitation, is clean.[5]

Something more is needed. One difference seems to lie in the link with ancestors, or in the new religious proscriptions of tobacco and cannabis. Unlike the traditional strains of tobacco, sugarcane grows most anywhere in the area, and it was never associated with ancestral homesteads or other fixed spots. And unlike tobacco and cannabis, sugarcane, coffee, and cotton are not objects of ecclesiastic disapproval.

The Gender Dimension

The kinds of property whose sale produces bitter money tend to be commodities whose sale benefits men more directly than women. In land, tobacco, and perhaps cannabis, it is the men who tend to receive the cash for the goods sold. This is so even though the labor of women may have outweighed that of the men in the farming.

This gender dimension is especially noteworthy. These are new ways of getting rich to which men have privileged access. They monopolize these transactions through superior contacts with government officials, with company representatives, and with distant city markets. The concentration of what was once family wealth into male hands, in cash, has proved especially dangerous to family welfare among the Luo, as in many other African societies where cash crops or other new sources have boosted incomes suddenly.

Several features of cash make it especially risky.[6] One is its *concealability*. Whereas in the past, one spouse could easily notice the other's taking food from the granary and challenge this, cash hides in pockets, and Luo men do not usually let their wives or children know how much they possess (see also Parkin 1980:207–208; Whisson 1964). Another feature is *divisibility*. Cash is more easily divisible than livestock when there is temptation to spend. (Livestock is a form of wealth more strongly associated with men anyway.) Finally, the *transportability* and almost universal *substitutability* (to economists, "fungibility") of cash make it easier to spend than other, older forms of wealth. All these features combine to produce what we may call a "private pocket syndrome," in which family members lose collective control over family wealth. The principle is widely observable in Africa. It would seem to be at the root of disturbing relationships between cash cropping and malnutrition that some observers have suggested in some areas where, though farmers may be accustomed to handling property of substantial value, there is no long tradition of handling it in large sums of cash.[7] What makes bitter money bitter, it would seem, is not simply that it represents foreigners and capitalism, but also that it represents an upset in the balance of control over wealth between the sexes. Men and women are not "equal," among the Luo, but there is a valued stability in family management that abrupt changes in income flows can damage.

Popular reconstructions of female suicide stories illustrated extreme cases of the disruption. In a case I knew in Kanyamkago location, a young woman, Acholla Anyango, and her husband grew a tobacco crop for the first time for the British-American Tobacco buying center. They had both worked hard on the crop, transplanting, weeding, spraying, and priming. As the time approached to sell part of the crop, the husband announced that when he sold the tobacco (as only men did), he planned to use the money toward a bridewealth payment for a second wife—or so he was said to have done. Soon Acholla Anyango drank a bottle of the tobacco pesticide. When discovered, she was rushed by road to the hospital, but she died within a few hours. The pattern of the story was familiar to locals, and where details were unclear, popular interpretation filled them in.[8]

Bitter money affects family fertility, a concern of both men and women. For men's misdeeds, women and children suffer with them, or even instead of them. Beliefs in bitter money thus would seem to give women an incentive to help safeguard their male relatives' property, to the extent that this is also *family* property.

The Luo have a general belief in "collective fate," such that lineage members expect all will be affected by an individual's breach of certain taboos. One manifestation is the concept of *chira*, considered to be a lethal wasting disease brought about by a major breach of norms concerning family order, notably in seniority relationships or marital fidelity (see Goldenberg 1982:143–146; Parkin 1978). My informants felt that the forbidden trade that produces bitter money does not produce or involve *chira*, at least not as a rule. From an outsider's perspective, however, the concepts both rest on a common assumption about responsibility. It is a double-edged principle: individual actions affect the welfare of the group, and so the group bears responsibility for the actions of the individual.

Are gender politics satisfactory in themselves to explain bitter money? Probably not quite. Gold, which yields bitter money, is sometimes sold by women as well as men. A stranger's lost money, when found, has no gender attached, yet it is similarly thought bitter. And on the other hand, sugarcane profits accrue almost entirely to men, though men and women may both contribute labor; yet sugar does not yield bitter money.

Age

An explanation in terms of age may help. Young men selling land, tobacco, or cannabis—all things the elders have controlled in the past—can often become richer than their fathers. This disturbs many Luo elders profoundly; it threatens their authority. It threatens, too, the authority that rests on the elder's right to allocate livestock for their sons' marriages, since junior men who deal in these commodities can now buy their own cattle.

But again, some of the facts are awkward. Gold today is mined, panned, and sold largely by elders, and this commodity yields bitter money too. Conversely, migrant wage labor has for generations enabled young men to earn more money than their fathers, but money earned this way is not thought bitter. An age explanation may help us understand bitter money, but it could not stand alone.[9]

Bitterness and Illegality

Is there a relation between the cultural and religious proscriptions we have seen, and the proscriptions of national law in Kenya? Some of the transactions that produce bitter money are in the part of the informal economy sometimes called "black market": traffic in cannabis and unlicensed traffic in gold are criminal offenses.

But tobacco is not illegal to grow or sell; nor, of course, are roosters. And by considering transactions that are illegal in national law, but are unconnected with "bitterness" in Luo belief, one can reconfirm that illegality in itself does not make a commodity "bitter" to the Luo. One such transaction is smuggling. Neither the illegal movement of maize or other foods across district lines, nor the commerce in many other goods across national borders, produces bitter money.[10] Nor is money from sales of locally brewed grain beer *(aput)* or distilled liquor *(chang'aa)* classified as bitter money, though the government's campaigns against the latter have been vigorous. Finally, money from prostitution in the towns does not appear to be thought bitter.

So the proscriptions of Kenyan national law and those of the Luo belief do not neatly coincide. In a sense the differences may reflect the cool feelings on the part of many of these geographically peripheral Kenyans toward national government. To rural people, in the aggregate, local alcohol represents an economically sensible alternative to patronizing the urban-based, government-controlled bottling breweries.[11] The wealth stays in the rural areas longer. (Local beer is also important for other associations with tradition and sociability, the beer having been drunk in the past at important convocations of elders for important decisions.) Local alcohol, smuggling, and prostitution are all untaxed. The lively flow of humans and goods across the national borders reflects the artificiality of the nation-state—a colonially created unit with no ethnic, linguistic, or religious basis—in the eyes of many western Kenyans and their neighbors.

The gender issue enters here too. Smuggling across national and district lines, liquor distilling, and prostitution are three of the principal means open to women for gaining access to cash in western Kenya, and they can be some of the most lucrative. In both the towns and the countryside, liquor preparation is almost entirely a women's concern. That these trades are excluded from the bitter-money category might suggest a tacit local acceptance of these female income-earning efforts, or some recognition of their earning value in a market-linked economy that discriminates sharply by sex.[12] Bitterness is largely about the money of men.

Bitterness and Christian Sin

Local Christian churches in South Nyanza forbid the use of cannabis as sinful, and most also forbid or restrict the use of tobacco. Could religious prohibition be at the root of "bitterness"? Here again, the evidence does not fit squarely. For land and roosters, both yielders of bitter money, are commodities to which the church dogmas appear indifferent. And prostitution, condemned by most or all churches in the region, does not produce bitter money.

Criteria Determining Bitterness: A Polythetic Class

In sum, there is no single element in common to all the kinds of transactions that yield bitter money, which cannot be found in some other kinds of transactions that do not. And no commodity yielding bitter money has all of the attributes associated with bitterness. Clearly no simple explanation of bitter money will do. Instead, there seems to be a set of recurring themes, no one of which needs to be present for a transaction to be classified as bitter. A commodity with all the traits we have identified with bitterness would be a product of the land, associated with ancestors and family, extracted by or for foreigners with unfair compensation, involving female labor but yielding disproportionate profits for men and especially young men, easily obtained in relation to its value, condemned as sinful in Christian churches, and perhaps illegal in national law. But there seems to be no such commodity (see Table 1).

To understand a phenomenon like this we need to resort to a form of classification in which no single attribute defines a class. This is what biological taxonomists call a "polythetic" or "polytypic" class and the philosopher Ludwig Wittgenstein called a "family likeness" (1958:17). Wittgenstein's metaphor illustrates the general idea: "the rope consists of fibres, but it does not get its strength from any fibre that runs through it from one end to another, but from the fact that there is a vast number of fibres overlapping" (1958:87). A biologist first defined a "polytypic" class formally this way (Beckner 1959:22, quoted in Needham 1975:353):

> A class is ordinarily defined by reference to a set of properties which are both necessary and sufficient (by stipulation) for membership in the class. It is possible, however, to define a group K in terms of a set G of properties f, f2, . . . fn in a different manner. Suppose we have an aggregation of individuals (we shall not yet call them a class) such that:
>
> 1) Each one possesses a large (but unspecified) number of the properties in G.
> 2) Each f in G is possessed by large numbers of these individuals and
> 3) No f in G is possessed by every individual in the aggregate.
>
> By the terms of (3), no f is necessary for membership in this aggregate; and nothing has been said to warrant or rule out the possibility that some f in G is sufficient for membership in the aggregate.

So if we have several objects, each of which has several attributes, allocated in this way:

Table 1
Some Attributes of Forbidden Commodities

	Commodities Associated with Bitter Money				Commodities not Associated with Bitter Money			
	Land	Tobacco	Cannabis	Gold	Sugarcane cotton	Smuggled goods	Local liquors	Sexual services (prostitution)
Produced from the land				●	●		●	
Associated with ancestors (and thus with descent groups)	●	●	●					
Associated with Europeans or Asians as an alienable commodity	●	●		●	●			?
Produced by men and women; sold by men	●	●	●		●			
Controlled by elders in the past; sold now by juniors	●	●	●					
Easy money, in relation to labor required		●	●	●		?		
Condemned by Christian churches		●	●				●	●
Illegal to produce or sell				●		●	●	●

Object	Attributes
1	a/b/c
2	b/c/d
3	c/d/e
4	d/e/f

we may come to recognize a "family resemblance" among them, and call them a kind of class, even though there is no single attribute that members all have in common, and no member that possesses all the attributes that define the class.[13] It is this kind of thought that I think lies behind the Luo notion of bitter money. This is a "sliding" category.[14]

There may be a lesson in this for economic anthropology. Just as the defining quality of bitter money is not to be found in any single attribute of the commodities that produce it, but only in several combined, perhaps the deeper explanation of bitter money—the real cause—is not to be understood with any one theoretical approach. Perhaps the causes are multiple (as causes, alas, so often are); and perhaps, moreover, they cannot be grasped within a single paradigm, like "diffusion," "function," or "cognitive structure." To understand a phenomenon like bitter money may require thinking in several ways at once.

Notes

1. As Wipper notes, the distinctions between nativistic, millenarian, prophetic and messianic movements, cargo cults, and crisis cults are fine and merging ones; these have much in common.

2. See Wipper 1977:43–44, 52, 70–71. She quotes Nyanza Provincial Commissioner John Ainsworth in 1908, and other Luo district authorities in the 1920s, on the dangers of popular cannabis smoking and the alleged associations between this smoking, on the one hand, and witchcraft, crime, and Mumbo-related Gusii hostilities toward the Administration, on the other.

3. Among the better known politico-religious revitalization movements in Kenya have been the active Dini ya Msambwa resistance movement in what are now Kakamega and Bungoma Districts in northern Nyanza Province, and of course the Mau Mau uprising in Central Province. (Cf. other variously comparable examples surveyed in D. Barrett 1968; D. Barrett et al. 1973; Fernandez 1978; and Ranger 1986.) African case material is adding to a broader anthropological literature on "revitalization" movements that has tended to focus on Melanesians and on Indians of the American West.

4. The combination of local and Judeo-Christian magico-religious systems in a complex of political protest is reminiscent of the Zion church Barolong boo

Ratshidi (Tshidi) of South Africa, described by Comaroff (1985). But these are themes common to revitalization movements in many parts of the world.

5. Cotton is a crop closely associated with aggressive foreign influence: in the early decades of this century the colonial government forced Luo farmers in the lower lands to grow it. Hut and poll taxes provided economic coercion; local agricultural extension agents provided physical coercion by beating farmers who refused to plant the crop.

6. See Simmel 1978, esp. chapt. 4 and 5; and Parkin 1980.

7. Messer (1984) includes a brief literature review on this topic; see also Fleuret and Fleuret (1980) on Kenya. (The results of recent field surveys by the International Food Policy Research Institute in South Nyanza and by P. Peters and others in Malawi should add further knowledge.) A policy implication is that large, lump sum cash payments for cash crops, land, or other resources, made to only a single representative of the family, may be a disservice to all in a society like this. Of course, where farmers have been accustomed for centuries to managing major amounts of cash, as in parts of West Africa or coastal East Africa, the conversion of family wealth into cash may have the reverse effect of facilitating savings and investments. Little is known about this.

8. Many Luo women resent acquiring co-wives—hence the term *nyiego*, jealousy, is the root of the term *nyieka*, co-wife—though not all. Seniority of marriage order is respected, some even encourage their husbands to marry again, because of the new labor that will come under the first wives' command. Wilson (1967) examines Luo suicides.

9. An interesting question for further research would be how women and elders *manipulate* the bitter money concept to further their own "category interests." Do they promote the concept to prevent sales of property in which they have partial interests? Ferguson (1985) raises similar questions in the case of Lesotho livestock.

10. Kanyamkago, near the Tanzanian border, saw much small-scale smuggling during my field research, at a time when the border was officially closed. Many Luo and Kuria had relatives on both sides of the border, whose homes provided convenient way stations, and many shopkeepers on both sides traded actively across the line. The main commodities that flowed from Kenya south into Tanzania were gasoline, beer, and simple manufactured items for household consumption, which the Tanzanian economy was having difficulty providing to the hinterland: soap, salt, sugar, matches, batteries, etc. Kenyan currency was also in demand in Tanzania. Northward, in exchange, flowed ox-plows, leather goods like shoes, cotton goods like sheets, some high-technology items including radios and tape recorders, and some packaged foods including honey and instant coffee. Staple foods flowed in both directions, depending on local supplies at any given time. Generally speaking, the Kenyan side of the border exhibited much more economic activity, at least in the towns, the difference being extremely stark in the evenly divided western border town of Isebania.

11. This does not, of course, imply that the local alcoholic beverages are preferable in all ways. Local grain beer has high nutritive value, but *chang'aa* has little and is popularly thought to be dangerous to the brain if improperly distilled.

12. Other interpretations are possible, however. Women's liquor-distilling, their prostitution, and often their smuggling serve men's needs and wants; and the exclusion of these from the bitter money category may be interpreted as a part of a general pattern of subjugation. Nor do earnings from prostitution benefit females alone; indeed, the service fees are commonly paid to male owners of bars and hotels and the women receive only a fraction.

13. Needham traces the roots of polythetic classification to the 18th-century French biologist Michel Adanson, but states that the "achievement" was not consummated until after 1950 (1975:353). "Polythetic" comes from the Greek *poly*, many; *thetos*, arrangement; the contrasting term is "monothetic." The use of the concepts in this work does not necessarily imply endorsement of Needham's broader views on the relation of anthropology to science, as they appear in sections IV and V of his article.

14. Some other Luo conceptual categories "slide" in simpler ways. For instance, term *jokakwaro*, which literally means "descendants of one grandfather," can telescope to mean a patrilineage several or even many generations deep. (Early European land adjudication officers in the area had trouble understanding this one; they sought to identify groups of a single size as "the *jokakwaro*".) The elements comprising bitter money differ not in scale, but in kind.

6

Bitter Money:
Some "Outmoded" Perspectives

Scriptural Prohibitions: A Diffusionist Approach

We have seen that not all the commodities associated with bitterness are forbidden in Christian churches in Luoland. To this extent, the complex of beliefs surrounding bitter money cannot be said to have been taken whole from foreign church influence. Could it be, though, that the basic distinction between good and evil wealth is a ruboff from missionaries and the Bible?

Numerous European and American church missions, and still more numerous independent Kenyan churches that have sprouted from them, have made the Bible available in Luoland, in Luo, Swahili, and English; and it is widely read. The Old Testament draws distinctions between ill-gained wealth and other wealth, warning that the former may not last in its owner's hands. The Book of Proverbs (dating from about 1,000 B.C.) contains these admonitions: "Treasures of wickedness profit nothing" (10:2); "A good man leaveth an inheritance to his children's children; and the wealth of the sinner is laid up for the just" (13:22); "Wilt thou set thine eyes upon that which is not? For riches certainly make themselves wings; they fly away as an eagle toward heaven" (23:5). The work ethic is an important part of honorable wealth: "The labour of the righteous tendeth to life: the fruit of the wicked to sin" (Proverbs 10:16); "Wealth gotten by vanity [in the New English version, 'quickly'] shall be diminished: but he that gathereth by labour shall increase" (13:11). Gaining wealth by evil means can lead to death: "So are the ways of every one that is greedy of gain; which taketh away the life of the owners thereof" (Proverbs 1:19). There is even something resembling the notion of "bitterness," which might be imagined to be connected with minerals like gold: "An ungodly man diggeth up evil: and in his lips there is as a burning fire" (Proverbs 16:27).

The New Testament is equally clear on private profit and greed, and explicit on the dangers of ill-gotten money. Moneychangers must be kept out of temples (John 2:14); and "the love of money is the root of all evil" (1 Tim. 6.10).[1] Judas Iscariot's betrayal or "sale" of Christ earns him thirty pieces of silver, which become, in some versions, an essential part of his violent end: "Now this man [Judas] purchased a field with the reward of iniquity; and falling headlong, he burst asunder in the midst, and all his bowels gushed out" (Acts 1:18).[2] Like Luo beliefs about bitter money, these biblical warnings all convey a sense of divine justice concerning the greedy. They also set firm boundaries between the salable and the unsalable.

The division of money into good and evil types in Nyanza suggests the influence of dualistic Christian religion as a root of the Luo response to money and market. An association of individualistic market behavior with the devil, in the bitter money complex, also suggests the Luo are somehow unwilling to accept both the profound foreign economic and religious influences together as a package. Response to economic change is pitched in a "Western" religious idiom, and vice versa.

To explain bitter money merely as a result of foreign religious influence, however, would leave big questions unanswered. Not only would the prohibitions on sales of land and roosters go unaccounted for, as noted earlier, but the larger question of *why* the Luo adopted beliefs about good and evil wealth once exposed to them would remain open. This is a central problem with any diffusionist explanation, and one that leads to questions about function.

Some Functional Explanations

At one level, the beliefs about bitter money would seem to serve explanatory, *psychological* functions.[3] Like the famous witchcraft beliefs of the Zande (Evans-Pritchard 1937), they help to account for misfortunes otherwise hard to understand. As some of my informants have told me, bitter money helps to explain why some young women have multiple miscarriages while others do not, why some children grow up as vagabonds and thieves while others do not, and why one farmer's cattle but not another's just sicken and die. And like the equally famous Trobriand Island canoe magic (Malinowski 1935), the *oso* rituals lend an element of human control to the great turns of fortune: if a ceremony is duly sponsored and correctly performed, it may not only prevent disaster but help the owner's family to prosper and multiply.[4] In adding a human dimension to the relations between the natural and supernatural, the beliefs would seem to allay anxieties about some of the most fundamental questions in Luo life. In doing so, however, they would seem to create other anxieties: they add mystical dangers and tensions to transactions that would otherwise be fairly straightforward.

Looking beyond the possible psychological or explanatory functions, one could hypothesize that bitter money serves *social* functions. Luo society tends strongly toward the gerontocratic. The invocation of ancestors in decisions about new wealth calls elders into play, for it is elders who are closest to ancestors and who are thought to communicate with them most easily. Belief in bitter money would seem to legitimize the elders' authority: it contributes to the elders' special domain of competence and power. It also legitimizes the churches and their leaders, since many have switched the agency behind bitter money from ancestral spirits to the devil and it is the church leaders and congregations who confront this threat. Elders and clerics are, among other things, agents of social control, and the existence of bitter money gives society a reason to continue holding them in respect.

Another possible functional explanation is *economic*. The belief in bitter money serves to regulate transactions. It restricts the alienation of land and may help prevent the accumulation of great wealth in a few hands. By this mode of reasoning, the beliefs may be based on either or both of two principles: egalitarianism (a concern to minimize differences in wealth) or risk averseness (a concern that no member of society should fall below a minimum level of livelihood). These principles are of course closely linked, since without some social constraints on accumulation, the richer members of any African agrarian society can progressively impoverish poorer ones by the mere economic advantages of their positions—for instance, they can afford to lend at interest, control the terms of share contracting agreements, serve as "pawnbrokers" for emergency grain sales, or buy up their neighbors' land in bad seasons. The knowledge that a transaction will produce bitter money gives the Luo pause before entering into it. Purification rituals *(oso)* are expensive and rather frightening; they involve powerful, dangerous, and unknown forces. And where they do occur, the purification rituals for transforming bitter money into good money would seem to serve a redistributive function, in that they ensure that new wealth is shared with guests and a ritual specialist. The rituals may also serve a purpose in merely bringing relatives and neighbors together (cf. Durkheim 1915). This latter Durkheimian explanation does not depend on economic principles like redistribution but may be considered in conjunction with them.

In another economic line of reasoning, one might suppose that beliefs about bitter money serve to minimize the accumulation of wives by men who have only the volatile earnings from land, gold, or tobacco for support. A snag with this approach is that in my data, much of the wealth from sales of tobacco is in fact used for buying cattle, despite the ideal that it be spent on other things. The real and the ideal do not match well enough for this explanation to hold by itself.

A problem with these explanations is the one that has dogged functionalist theorists since Radcliffe-Brown. How does society decide what it "wants," and see that it happens? If one assumes that individual thought and behavior conform to society's norms for society's benefit, and that they do so for this purpose, one should be able to show just how society (1) decides, consciously or unconsciously, what it needs or wants, and (2) exerts its will over the individual. Both are hard problems. Even if we accept that reciprocity or redistribution can somehow benefit Luo society, and that society can train its individuals to act in these ways (say, through the attraction of ceremonies, through fears of witchcraft accusations, or through semantic categories), we are faced with the question of how society determines that this leveling behavior is right to begin with. (If no one shared wealth, would the society starve to extinction? A hard case to prove.)

But our inability to spot a mechanism by which society determines what is good for itself and implements it does not necessarily mean we must reject the notion of functions altogether. Regardless of how belief in bitter money arises, or is perpetuated, it may indeed help allay fears about diseases, reconfirm the status of elders, inhibit foolish alienations of land, and restrict the processes concentrating wealth into fewer hands. Even where functional explanations cannot pinpoint an institution's causes, they may still help to identify its effects. The dangers lie in mistaking effects for causes, or trying too hard to portray these as circularly self-reinforcing.

Cognitive Explanations: Spheres of Exchange

One way of analyzing beliefs in bitter money is to conceive of the Luo economy as divided into "spheres of exchange" (cf. Barth 1967; Bohannan 1955, 1959), one for permanent lineage property and one for other property. Writing on Lesotho, James Ferguson (1985) has suggested, like others before him elsewhere in Africa, that similar spheres are separated by a one-way barrier: cash is convertible to cattle, but not vice versa. In these terms, the Luo would appear to have a two-way barrier between their "spheres." Like Sotho men, Luo men try to prevent conversions of cattle or land into cash or other forms in which women gain better claims over them: this state is what Ferguson has called a "domain of contestation." At the same time, however, the beliefs about bitter money ostensibly prohibit Luo men from using just any money to buy cattle or land for their patrilineages. But today, at least, the barrier is semipermeable: land or livestock may be rented out for money, and money can be ritually purified for buying land or livestock.

Part of what separates money and other commodities would seem to be a distinction between what is subjectively appreciated and socially embedded, and what is counted and socially unattached. Like many other Africans south of the Sahara, Luo consider counting people or livestock an antisocial act, a breach of etiquette.[5] It dries out flesh and blood to a talliable quantum.[6] Like enumerating people, selling commodities associated with relatives and ancestors seems to Luo an unnatural reduction.

Further Cognitive Explanations: Anomaly and Liminality

Bitter money is an unusual medium of exchange. It falls between ordinary categories, and it is perhaps this that makes it dangerous (Douglas 1966). A sale that converts the fixed and inalienable (the ancestral graves and the land) into the quintessentially movable commodity, money, has breached a fundamental distinction. So has a transaction that reduces quality to quantity, or a personal relationship to an impersonal one.

Commodities that yield bitterness are ones that breach or transcend ordinary categories themselves. Tobacco is grown on the spot where a homestead was, but is no longer. This is not the domestic sphere but not the wilderness either. Tobacco smoke to the Luo is neither air nor water, but something of both. The rooster crows between day and night, dividing sleep from waking time; to the Luo it also stands at the frontier of civilization and wilderness. Bitter money is held in the hands of the living, but watched over by spirits of the dead: it comes from involving the sacred in commerce that is profane. It mediates what the Luo think of as their old, group-based redistributive modes of livelihood, and what they see as the new, individualistic mode of the market. Cash is a paradoxical joiner:

> Money . . . divides into two alternate ways—spiritual and worldly . . . in money are both the inherent tendency to split into spirit and matter and the possibility to hold them together. [Hillman 1982:34, 38]

More than just any money, bitter money seems to reinforce such divisions while bridging them.

Bitter money and the surrounding complex of beliefs suggest a fascination with the cyclical dimensions of life, and with contradictions they contain. The land is a "magician" because it both feeds us and devours us. Luo cite this as a reason why humans must not sell land; land is something with powers beyond human understanding or control. And there is a sense of respect and justice toward the land. The bride cannot be procured by exchanging away lineage land, because on coming into the lineage she would have to eat the products of the same land. Tobacco, like land, involves mystical cycles of its own: the bride procured in fire and smoke will perish in fire and smoke. The smoker who sees an ancestor is likely to see him or her smoking too. Bitter money of any kind, if ritually purified, will keep returning to its owner's homestead . . . not like a bad penny, for the Luo, but like a good one.

The Europeans whose religions have been spliced together with indigenous beliefs to produce today's bitter money beliefs may themselves be seen as anomalous, enigmatic creatures. While they appear as missionaries preaching brotherly love and sharing, many of them live in isolated mission compounds, with the first fences in their neighborhoods. While they instruct about equality, they dress and eat unlike peasant farmers, keep fancy vehicles these local people cannot afford, and educate just a few privileged local sons for lucrative salaried futures. The disjunctions between white ideals and white behavior, and between the European and African cultures generally, are harsh realities that bitter money beliefs would seem both to express and to try to control.

But these interpretations can be pushed too far, and the problem is that we seldom know when we have done so. Spheres of exchange, liminality, and the cosmic paradoxes may sometimes exist only in discourse or interpretation. Every African society doubtless has some individuals who privately suppose they can transfer any commodity in any direction they want, who are quite happy to live with some ambiguity, and who are not particularly puzzled by positive or negative feedback loops. Some may suppose their *own* society's cultural emphasis on ancestors, lineage, and livestock controlled by elders to be something like "false consciousness" or mystification, continually maintained by local-born male elders, even while they play along with it in practice. Private ideology tempers and qualifies public ideology, and vice versa; and these can contradict each other. Cognitive categories may not be static: Luo or any other humans may modify them or formulate new ones as the commodities in their lives take on new meanings, and this very fluidity defies verification. Finally, spheres of exchange or liminal mediators sometimes appear as figments of the anthropological imagination, one inclined to build on received theory as well as on recorded fact, and to create order on paper where order is hard to find *in situ*.[7] All cognitive interpretation is debatable; interpretation itself is a "domain of contestation."

Complementarities

To begin to explain why the Luo concept of bitter money exists, we have adopted several perspectives. At the simplest, some contemporary approaches, including political economy approaches highlighting resistance, and others based on gender and age, suggest *whose interests* the belief serves. They may also reveal how people of some groups or categories manipulate it. Among classic anthropological orientations, to simplify again, diffusionism asks *from whom* the belief came. Functionalism asks *what good* the belief does for the people who hold it. Cognitive structural analysis asks *how the elements fit together* in coherent meaning, and why they have been chosen in the first place.

None of the answers can be fully known. So none of the questions that "why" covers is wholly useless or indispensable. Each of the theoretical perspectives—political economy, diffusionism, functionalism, structuralism—yields a part of an understanding that will always be incomplete.[8] And in the end, none of these schools of thought can truly debunk another, because no two ask "why" the same way.

A Recurring Theme

The motley assortment of commodities yielding bitter money suggests that no simple explanation for the belief will suffice. But there is a recurring theme. The Luo perceive a problem in the rise of possessive individualism. The theme emerges regularly, both in informants' discussions of their beliefs and their meanings (the "emic," or insiders' perspectives) and in the comparative analysis of the symbols and behavior involved (the "etic," or outsiders' perspectives). Bitter money is a fluid category. The commodities to which it refers probably vary from one time and place to another, and the concept may thus provide a window on what economic changes the members of the society consider harmful or dangerous. Tracking the changes through time and space is a task for further research. The Luo country in the early 1980s was undergoing rapid social and economic change, and the bitter money concept pointed to specific perceived threats to family and community. There are no rules, often, until they are broken; and taboos on purchases and sales reflect real exchanges that the Luo consider in one sense or another as betrayals.

It is not all individualism that society reacts against with these cultural sanctions. Rather, it is self-indulgence in unaccustomed or newly politicized contexts: in forms of property in which group membership has entitled other individuals to overlapping claims in the past. It is the individual usurpation of benefits, and symbols, for which others have lived and worked. Whom transgressors are betraying depends on the circumstances, and on interpretation. It can be family or lineage, or perhaps even neighborhood or ethnic group. It can be ancestors, a debt to whom one can repay only by handing on an inheritance to the future. In the abstract, the principle of betrayal is the same; at this level, bitter money is a monothetic class. In the 20th century the Luo have tasted money and private property as never before, and refused to swallow these ideas whole.

Notes

1. Yet in Western economic philosophies, the evil of self-interested profit is also sometimes seen as the root of all good, as in the philosophies of Adam Smith and Bernard Mandeville (for a discussion see Macfarlane 1985:73). Crump (1981) compares several of the world's most popular religions in their classification of money (pp. 284–289). Parkin (1985) presents anthropological treatments of philosophies of evil and good in a variety of societies.

2. The field became known as the field of blood, and became taboo: in some versions, it was used thereafter for burying foreigners. The money, of course, had come from foreigners to begin with.

3. Here there is only space to suggest possible psychological functions of direct relevance to anthropology. For discussions of the "depth psychology" of money, from Jungian perspectives, see Lockhart et al. (1982).

4. As Beattie (1966) and others have argued, however, the expressive and dramatic functions of ritual are at least as important as the instrumental (or the explanatory) ones; rituals *say* things as well as *do* things. These purposes can merge. As with cargo cults and ghost dances, "it is the ritual dance or other performance itself . . . that it is believed or hoped will be effective" (p. 70). Rituals like these "are recourses, in times of stress, to the consolations of rite and drama" (p. 71).

5. The aversion of counting humans and animals spans the continent. It is a central recurring theme, for instance, in Sembene Ousmane's Senegalese novel *God's Bits of Wood:* the title is taken from a euphemism some Senegalese use for human beings when counting them.

6. To historically minded western Kenyans, counting people or livestock also connotes sizing up a group for a battle or raid. Interestingly, though Luo dislike the idea of counting people, one of their favorite books of the Old Testament is the Book of Numbers, in which such counts fill pages. Luo deem round numbers bad omens. In bridewealth and other special transactions, 100 is likely to become 99 or 101.

7. It is not always realized how many of the great theories of social and cultural anthropology have been based on little or no firsthand field observation. Some major works of Emile Durkheim, Max Weber, James George Frazer, Marcel Mauss, Arnold van Gennep, Ruth Benedict, and Claude Lévi-Strauss are cases in point.

8. Of course, some explanations may be more incomplete than others. As a Luo lawyer once told me, "the answer to every question is, 'it depends.' "

7

African and Latin American Comparisons

Some African Variations

Luo beliefs about bitter money are perhaps unusually elaborate in their associations with spirits and demons, with lineages, and with bridewealth. But the Luo are not unusual in Africa in their cultural response to new forms of possessive individualism, as the Fipa example in Tanzania showed. Other aspects of the bitter money complex find parallels elsewhere south of the Sahara. Examples from isolated sources, to be taken with caution, suggest some of the variations to be explored.

In Malawi, Chewa farmers in a tobacco-growing area are reported to believe, like the Luo, that money they make this way will disappear faster than other money.[1] The Malawians appear not to explain this special quality of tobacco money by reference to spiritual associations, but more simply in terms of the lump sum cash payments they receive for the crop.[2] This is, as seen earlier, a part of the Luo explanation too.

In some parts of Africa, inherited land is not deemed properly salable but other land is.[3] In the 1930s, Gunter Wagner noted among the Maragoli Luhya that the transferability of land depended on whom it came from. Land from a (paternal) grandfather was less transferable than land from one's father (Wagner 1956:77–78), and this, in turn, was less transferable than land one had cleared for the first time, which could be freely sold.[4]

In various parts of West Africa, similarly, ethnographers have documented popular distinctions between inherited and other properties affecting their salability, and occasionally suggested that there are links between sources of wealth and the purposes for which it may be disposed. One case comes from a plateau in the Fiata area of southeastern Togo, among members of the Gen, Anloa, and Peda ethnic groups described in an unpublished ethnography by M. C. Litoux-Le Coq (1974) cited by E. Le Bris (1979:110–111). Lands, under increasing competition, are divided into parallel strips corresponding regularly to lineages (as among the Luo and their Luyha and Gusii neighbors). Competition for holdings has made claims hard to trace to original settling ancestors, and chiefs take the responsibility of directing devolution and dispute settlement among free or "slave" strangers who have individually gained a foothold in the territory. The situation is far from one of indivisible or collective group rights. But the authors draw our attention to restrictions on land sale, mortgage, and rental that become tighter as the transaction becomes more important.

> Not all justifications [that the "owner" might invoke] are accepted [by the family]. . . . Those considered most valid are marriage payments, tribunal payments, a child's school expenses, or a profitable investment like a maize mill; but the purchase of a bicycle, a trip, and the construction of a house are purposes systematically rejected. [Litoux-Le Coq, cited in Le Bris 1979:110; my translation]

Le Bris continues,

> Any alienation of a patrimony occasions a ceremony, as if the one responsible for the action wished to be pardoned a misdeed before the fact. [p. 110; my translation]

Beyond this intriguing tidbit, no further information is relayed. From the reports of Antheaume (1974) on the village of Agbetiko in the same region, however, Le Bris reports, "the peasants alienate first, by preference, the parcels their fathers or grand-fathers bought" (presumably rather than the ones these forebears inherited).[5]

In much of Africa south of the Sahara, similar thinking about inheritance and salability often applies to livestock. In Wa, northern Ghana, Polly Hill has found that Dagarti people distinguish between inherited cattle as subject to the approval of relatives before sale, and other cattle as freely exchangeable (Hill 1970:139).

Ghana provides cases of beliefs that roughly parallel Luo "bitter money" in several ways. In 1940 Margaret Field described beliefs and customs concerning money among the Ga agricultural and fishing townspeoples, some of whom were adopting cocoa farming as one of their main money-earning activities. She noted two-sided feelings toward money, noting an informant's words, "money is a most wonderful thing" (p. 218) but also reporting, " 'It is money that is spoiling our towns,' is a remark that elders often make" (1940:214).

Field explains the "association in people's minds between money and the supernatural, and this mostly among the men" (p. 218), in a cash-cropping area:

> I was once staying, in pursuit of some facts about witchcraft, in a forest-country village where most of the people did some cocoa-farming and cocoa-trading. Every one of them had an *aye* (nonkilling witchcraft) for making money. It worked thus. A man who had this power might meet a stranger and notice him to be wearing twenty pounds' worth of gold ornaments. By his witchcraft he would then "suck" out the essence *(eno emli nii)* of the stranger's gold. When the stranger reached his own town he would find twenty pounds' worth of expenses or fines waiting for him, or would in some other manner be forced to part with twenty pounds. The *aye* in the other town would find a windfall of twenty pounds coming to him from some surprising direction. He must not "eat" (enjoy or spend) any of this windfall, but must treat it as capital and invest it or trade with it. With its profits he must be generous and must give away to anyone in need an equal amount to that originally "sucked" from the stranger. If he were to "eat" any of the original twenty pounds "sucked" from the stranger, he would become an *obeyefo* (a killer-witch who cannot stop killing) and would have to join flesh-feasting bands of other wicked killers. [1940:218–219][6]

Note several similarities to the Luo case: the cash cropping; the link between how one obtained money and how one may dispose of it; the requirement that ill-gotten wealth must be generously shared; and the oral imagery of "sucking" and "eating" money (as in Luo "eating" the land by eating its blessings, or as in "eating" a bribe or tasting "bitterness").

The Ashanti peoples, also of Ghana, have held beliefs about tainted wealth, and at least some of these still hold, according to sources interviewed.[7] It is thought that money gained by selling or mortgaging valued family property, including a home, or inherited gold objects or other heirlooms, may not be used for marriage transactions. These transactions include not just bridewealth, paid from the groom's family to the bride's, but also the "trousseau" of property a bride brings into a marriage. Nor may this ill-gained wealth be used to contribute to birth rituals or funerals (used for coffins, for instance) without angering ancestral spirits and thus endangering people and property. In short, it must be kept apart from sacred occasions. It is not just the one who disposes of the property who may be affected, but also the recipient and others connected with both. What harm will befall transgressors cannot be predicted.

As the Ashanti have a long and well-known history of matriliny, they add a new dimension unseen in the case of the patrilineal Luo. The Ashanti kingdom, in some ways a centralized empire up to colonial times (see Busia 1951; Wilks 1967), also adds an important dimension in political hierarchy. Rules about evil money are applied at high levels. Among these Ghanaians, symbols of chiefly office or "stool property" were not salable: headbands and armbands, gold ornaments on sandals, ritual musical instruments, or linguist's staffs, etc.—none of these, of course, were considered a leader's personal property anyway (cf. Busia 1951:66, 70). According to two members of the Busia family, selling them would have yielded dangerous money, which again would have to be kept apart from sacred ceremonies. Here the polity as a whole would be betrayed, and it might suffer altogether as a consequence of the misdeed.

The concept of capital as fruitful or barren capital is apparently familiar among Hausa traders in Nigeria, who refer to capital as *uwa* (mother). The ethnographer Yusuf writes,

> A fertile capital *(uwa mai amfani)* is one which ideally "gives birth to issues," in other words, marginal profit . . . or reproduces itself manifold. An "ominous capital" *(jarin tsiya)* is, on the other hand, one which leads to the total bankruptcy of the trader who initially invests it. [Yusuf 1975:169]

Yusuf does not tell what is thought to make the capital "fertile" or "ominous."

In some West African schools of Islamic thought, if not in Islamic thought across the continent, money or wealth acquired from any of a variety of prohibited activities must not be used for holy purposes, for instance to finance a *hajj* (pilgrimage to Mecca). Beliefs I collected in the Gambia illustrate the point. These come mainly from Mandinka-speaking informants—members of an ethnic group that Islam has influenced in waves since the 14th century. Similar beliefs may be found among Fula, Wollof, and other peoples of the region.[8]

Particularly forbidden in these and other Muslim traditions is the use of money from usury (Arabic, *ribā*, literally "increase" or "excess")—a sin many local believers consider second only to murder in gravity—for the holy acts. As elsewhere in the Islamic world, what exactly constitutes *ribā* is a topic of hot debate. Some think *any* interest on a loan qualifies, others only interest at exorbitant ratios or rates. The Qur'an expressly forbids "doubling," which many interpret to mean 100% interest.[9] Of course, as in other Islamic societies, many ruses have evolved for disguising interest charges on loans as gifts, or as sales and countersales.[10] But many fear (as many Luo fear about "laundered" bitter money) that the divine will not be fooled. As a young man explained a common Gambian worry, one who enjoys or "eats" the rewards of *ribā* is certain to fall ill: one's belly will swell up, and one will end up with vultures pulling out one's intestines.

Money from *ribā* is not the only evil money for the Mandinko: also evil is money from usurped inheritance, and, to some, money from extortion, murder, or other crimes against persons. It is all called *kodi jawo*, bad money (from Mandinka *kodoo*, money or silver, and *jawo*, variously meaning evil, ill-willed, enemy, or adversary). As some informants have explained it, *kodi jawo* is money one has not earned with one's own sweat, or from any wholehearted and legitimate contributions by others. No *hajj* performed with such wealth, it is said, can yield any spiritual reward. This wealth is also not for use on one's own family: one should not marry with it, sponsor a funeral, or build a family compound.

Some consider that a charity tithe (Arabic, *zakāt;* Mandinka, *jakko*) given to the poor from *kodi jawo* will never benefit one spiritually, as charity from honestly earned wealth does.[11] And wealth taken from one's earnings or harvests and earmarked for a charity tithe is considered in a sense like *kodi jawo*, unusable for one's personal or family life, and safeguarded by the threat of spiritual punishment.

Mandinko and neighboring Gambians believe that if an individual sells family land or other jointly inherited property to purchase goods for personal profit and prestige, without the consent of the co-heirs, the new property will come to no good.[12] To illustrate, in the Lower River Division of the Gambia, the story was recounted of a man staying in the city of Serrekunda, who had sold his inherited home compound in 1984. As it happened, his mother had warned him not to sell; in a frightening dream, she had envisaged him in a smoky house. He reassured her that he intended to buy more land and houses for the family. But instead, he used the money to buy himself a car. Before long the car was completely smashed up. The man lost the rest of the money in the gambling casino by Kotu Beach, near the capital; then he fell ill.

In analyzing the story, informants said that the man should not have sold the cows for a selfish purpose like buying a car, but that some other purposes would have justified the sale: family food, ceremonies for circumcision, marriage, or perhaps naming an infant. They needed to be uses that would enhance family honor, not just the man's own personal glory.[13]

The rewards of betrayal are dangerous, in West African as in East African traditions, and in Muslim and Christian as in indigenous beliefs. In the Gambia, as in Kenya, enjoyment of wealth is spoken of as "eating" it—"consumption" is the convenient English term—eating forbidden wealth causes internal bodily harm. The Gambian's picture of the vultures pulling out the intestines is vaguely reminiscent of the Judeo-Christian image of Judas Iscariot's end, with his bowels gushing out upon his ill-earned field. The innards are turned out as if they no longer belonged to one: as if to repay a greater force or being—divinity, perhaps, or society.

Some Gambian Mandinko profess a belief that money from selling red peppers should not be used toward a *hajj*. Their color and hotness (the Mandinka term *kandi*, hot, refers to temperature or spiciness) are associated with hellfire, and peppers therefore are not to be mixed up with a holy mission. Hot pepper trade is rather stigmatized altogether, but it is thought particularly dangerous to steal hot peppers, or money or other wealth deriving from them: one will suffer a serious illness, lose a spouse or child, or perish in fire; and if one dies then, one will go to Hell. The beliefs may be tied to a local Muslim oral tradition about hot peppers. In this story, a mischievous angel tried to defy the word of the Prophet Muhammad when the latter proclaimed, one very wet day, that anything planted then would germinate. The angel planted a piece of hot coal. But the coal did indeed germinate: what grew, fittingly, was a hot pepper plant. The Prophet had the last word.[14]

Of course, in practice, some Gambian Muslims *do* use money from interest-bearing loans, or from pepper sales, for sacred and holy purposes like the *hajj*. Their neighbors say the pilgrims will receive the title of *haji,* but not the blessing. The achievement will be hollow.

Islamic beliefs have blended richly with indigenous religions, in the Gambia, and the agency by which *kodi jawo* comes to no good is variously conceived of as Allah or as ancestral spirits of a lineage. While strict Muslims insist it is Allah, others say it may be either. The thoughts about money tempered by concurrent beliefs from the great and little traditions are somewhat reminiscent of those found among the Christianized Luo, across the continent in Kenya. For Mandinko (as for Luo), how one obtained money determines how one may use it, and the links between source and purpose are charged with moral significance. The specific prohibitions on earning and on spending differ in these contexts, but the underlying principles are much alike. Betrayal and unfairness are common themes. In the Gambia, as in Ghana and in Kenya, evil money and the spiritual forces behind it help account for many misfortunes and mysterious turns of fate. They explain why one brother may sicken and die and another remain healthy, and why some roofs are torn off in storms, while others nearby, no better built, are not.

Latin American Comparisons

The ritual transformation of money between good and evil states, or between sacred and profane categories, has been observed in some societies having both semimonetized economies and semi-Christianized religious systems, in Central and South America. Most notable in this respect are beliefs about the baptism of money, as reported in Mitla, Mexico (Parsons 1936:90, 322), Los Boquerones, Panama (Gudeman 1976:202–204), and the southern Cauca Valley, Colombia (Taussig 1980: chapt. 7). Though Luo beliefs about bitter money do not appear to involve baptism, the Latin American reports provide some intriguing comparisons to the Luo case, telling in both the similarities and differences.

In each of these parts of Central and South America, the ethnographers have reported beliefs about the duplicitous baptism of money by godparents-to-be in Catholic baptismal ceremonies. In each, the godparent-to-be conceals a piece of money during the ceremony, and the piece is thought to be baptized, either in addition to the baby (Parsons 1936) or instead of it (Gudeman 1976:202; Taussig 1980:126).[15] After the baptized coin is spent, it returns to its owner, perhaps with other money, rather as Luo money, once ritually transformed, can return to its owner. According to Stephen Gudeman, a godparent in Santiago, Panama, is expected to throw out coins to unrelated children at the entrance of the church at the end of the ceremony, as though to prove that these are worthless and thus that he has not committed the evil deed.[16]

Michael Taussig further discusses contracts that Cauca Valley inhabitants are thought to make with the Devil to get rich. These farming people, of African descent, have become involved in a cash economy through a severe maldistribution of landholdings and an enclosure of land, through the establishment of large sugarcane plantations and wage labor, and through the spread of other smallholder cash crops like coffee and cocoa to supplement the food crops they grow on their own farms.[17] Straddling the gap between what Taussig (following Marx) has called precapitalist and capitalist modes of production, the Cauca Valley citizens maintain a perspective on both. It is this perspective, according to Taussig, that leads them to identify the devil with capitalism.

This is how Taussig describes the devil contracts (1980:13–14):

> Among the displaced Afro-American peasants who are employed as wage workers by the rapidly expanding sugarcane plantations in Colombia are some who are supposed to enter into secret contracts with the devil in order to increase their production and hence their wage. Such a contract is said to have baneful consequences for capital and human life. Moreover, it is believed to be pointless to spend the wage gained through the devil contract on capital goods such as land or livestock because these wages are inherently barren: the land will become sterile, and the animals will not thrive and will die. Likewise, the life-force in the plantation's inventory, the sugarcane, is rendered barren, too: no more cane will sprout

from a ratoon cut by a cane cutter who has entered into a devil contract. In addition, it is also said by many persons that the individual who makes the contract, invariably a man, will die prematurely and in pain. Short-term monetary gain under the new conditions of wage labor is more than offset by the supposed long-term effects of sterility and death.

From this and other passages in Taussig's book, one may gather that the Cauca Valley inhabitants have several things in common with the Luo. Both have been partially incorporated into a cash-based economy, largely by alien interventions. Both peoples have partially, but not wholly, embraced Christianity, mixing elements of it with local beliefs and practices. Both now divide money into good and evil kinds, associating the evil type with the devil. They appear to be associating the devil with market principles. Both consider the evil money as "barren," sterilizing, and ultimately destructive of family welfare. They believe that one must not seek to obtain land, crops, animals, or children by it (see Taussig 1980:13–14, 94–95, 99, 133). Both consider it morally wrong to gain profit through some forms of private property without working (see Taussig 1980:96). Both believe that evil money carries with it the destructive qualities with which it is imbued. But in both cases, money is ritually convertible to a form that will "stick" to its owner, or continually return (Taussig 1980:126–128).

But the differences between the Cauca Valley and the Luo beliefs about evil money are just as notable as the similarities. The Luo conceive of evil money in terms of potential damage to a lineage. Their beliefs are couched in an idiom familiar in Africa: one of ancestral spirits, bridewealth, intergenerational pressures, and the ideal cohesiveness of large unilineal kin groups.[18]

By contrast, the Cauca Valley Colombians conceive of evil money in terms of damage to an individual or a small family. Taussig and the other Latin Americanist ethnographers who report on good and evil money do not mention ancestors: the peoples they study, all having bilateral kinship systems, do not have the same concerns with intergenerational continuities in family or with the solidarity of large permanent kin groups. Instead, they have more pronounced concerns with fictive kinship in the *compadrazgo* pattern. Ritual coparenthood and godparenthood serve as supplementary links in a bilateral system, variously permitting social "insurance" links for emergencies, patronage for political or economic favors, and channels for intimacies beyond what kinship provides.

Beliefs about bitter money thus reflect the difference between a segmentary lineage system in the Luo case, and a bilateral kinship system in the Cauca Valley case.[19] Magico-religious beliefs appear closely tied into the fabric of social organization. While neither beliefs nor social behavior can be pointed to as a sure cause of the other, there is some logical consistency and fit between them.

The transformation of money takes very different forms in the African and Latin American contexts. In the Luo case, money is transformed by purification in a specific rite of apparently local provenance, performed in the company of visitors. The transformation of money is a sociable act. In the Cauca Valley and in some other Latin American settings, money is transformed by perversion of a Christian ritual, in secret. This is an antisocial act. But in both African and Latin American contexts, the transformation of money involves human mediation between the spiritual and the natural worlds. In both it involves local adaptations of Christianity for local purposes. In both, new market principles introduced by outsiders are clearly portrayed as dangerous.

Contracts with the Devil for wealth are a feature of Bolivian mining communities as described by June Nash (1979) and by Taussig, who here relies mainly on her work (Taussig 1980: part III). As mining plays an important part in Luo beliefs about bitter money, there may be reason for comparing their beliefs with the Bolivian mine workers'. Unfortunately this cannot be attempted in detail here, but on the face of it there are some parallels. Among Bolivian miners as among the Luo, an indigenous spirit and latterly the Devil of Christian belief are closely tied to a powerful new economic system to which the population has had trouble adjusting. Here again, it is by sacrifice that humans participate in the relations between the spiritual and natural worlds: the Bolivian miners' offering of a llama expresses their dependence on these forces and also represents an attempt to secure their bounty and their protection from mine disasters. And here again, there is an apparent fascination with cycle and paradox in humans' relations to the means of production. The informant's quotation that gives Nash's book her title is "We eat the mines and the mines eat us": this is why sacrifices to the spirit of the mines are necessary. It parallels with uncanny closeness the Luo woman's statement that "the land feeds us and swallows us," as her reason why the Luo must not sell land.[20]

In Bolivia as in western Kenya, the mines represent a new economic order incomprehensible in indigenous terms. They grew up as an extractive industry in two senses: extracting minerals from the ground and extracting labor from local people. Unfortunately I cannot agree fully with Taussig's portrait of the Bolivian mines or the Colombian sugar plantations as a coercive force into which the local people have been drawn against their will. In those places, as in Kenya, there are elements of local volition too behind workers' participation in these industries.[21] But in any of these contexts, the devil beliefs represent an ambivalence about the incursions of foreign cultures in religious and economic life.

Future study will doubtless tell more about why exchange taboos and mystical attributions to money arise in different forms, and in some settings but not others. These are cultural responses to changes often studied as economic or political phenomena. It is often in subtle cultural expressions—in songs, myths, religious imagery—that social maladjustments or hardships are most visible.[22] The links between particular people and particular property, and the links people perceive between how they acquire wealth and how they dispose of it, can serve as entry points into their sentiments about social change.

Notes

1. Pauline Peters, personal communication, December 1987, based on research in Lilongwe in 1986–87.

2. Reportedly, tobacco money is thought similar in this respect to money from labor migrants to South Africa. Men both remit this money or bring it back with them on return.

3. Meek (1946) remains a useful, though now dated, general source on African rules and conventions concerning land sales.

4. Moore (1986:267–283), writing on the Chagga of Tanzania, gives cases of people who sold land and were ostracized by their lineages or met violence.

5. Le Bris 1979:111. The translation is mine. Agbetiko too contains a wide ethnic mix, including an Adja-Fon majority led by a Toughban chiefly minority.

6. Field observes that the Ga money-making witchcraft (*aye*) "operates without tangible medicines and apparatus and without spoken words. It is project by the silent, invisible action of the witch's will alone" (1940:218n). In this limited respect it resembles some kinds of Luo witchcraft, including *sihoho*, or power of the evil eye (this, however, may not provide material reward to the witch).

7. The following information on Ashanti beliefs about tainted money comes from interviews with Naa-Morkor Busia and Abena Busia in June 1988. Some of the information, they have said, also applies to nearby Ga groups.

8. Based on my research in the Gambia in April and May 1987, and July through October 1988.

9. See especially Sura II, "The Cow": Verse 275: "Those who swallow [charge] usury cannot rise up as he ariseth whom the devil has prostrated by (his) touch. That is because they say: Trade is just like usury: whereas Allah permitteth trade and forbiddeth usury. . . . As for him who [refraineth and] returneth [to usury]—Such are rightful owners of the Fire. They will abideth

therein." Verse 276: "Allah hath blighted usury." Or see the Sura of "The Family of 'Imran'," Verse 130: "O Ye who Believe! Devour not usury, doubling and quadrupling . . . and ward off from [yourself] the Fire prepared for disbelievers."

10. See Rodinson (1974:35–43), and sources cited there, for well-documented Muslim ways of disguising interest charges that have been practiced in various societies since medieval times. This source is also a standard work on the broader topic of capitalism in Islamic belief and practice. See also Cardahi (1955:527–534) on Islamic law on usury.

11. On this point, however, local Gambian Qadiri Islamic beliefs seem to be at variance with some other Islamic traditions elsewhere. Schacht (1984:145) states that in Sunni Islamic belief (contrary to Gambian beliefs as reported to me), wealth from "unjustified enrichment" [Arabic, *faḍl māl bilā 'iwaḍ*], of which *ribā* is a special instance, *must* be given to the poor as a charitable gift. In another detail concerning *ribā*, Gambian beliefs differ from those he describes: for instance, Gambian informants consider *ribā* to include usurious nonmonetary loans, whereas Schacht defines it as "a monetary advantage without a countervalue which has been stipulated in favour of one of the two contracting parties in an exchange of two monetary values" (p. 145). Of course, *ribā* is a topic of centuries of debates in the Muslim world.

12. According to some Mandinko, the only purposes for which one may sell family cattle are for family food, or for sacred rites like circumcision celebrations or marriages.

13. Some added that motor vehicles and other machines do not "like" evil people, for instance drivers who visit prostitutes or who do not bathe. All put inside them must be spiritually in order; wealth put inside them must be achieved by one's own sweat.

14. However, some Mandinko, including some knowledgeable marabouts, claim never to have heard the idea that wealth from selling hot peppers cannot be used for a *hajj*. And others do not know the story of the coal.

15. Note the "image of limited good," as termed by George Foster (1965), or, in economists' terms, the assumption of a "zero-sum game." One's gain is sometimes popularly assumed to be tied to another's loss. The case of money-witching among the Ga of Ghana, described above, showed a similar assumption.

16. Parsons reports from Mitla that it is women who secretly baptize money, but Gudeman reports from Santiago, and Taussig from Cauca Valley, that it is men. However, these are only reports about beliefs; it may be that no one actually carries out the act.

17. That the subjects of Taussig's study are of African descent does not necessarily suggest any direct communicational links to the African beliefs described herein. The evidence is far too scanty for any such conclusions. There might, however, be some parallel interpretations of the Judeo-Christian Bible occurring.

18. It may be that the new prominence of the Devil, rather than angry ancestral spirits, as the main destructive force in Luo beliefs about bitter money reflects a decline in the importance of kinship as churches assume new

functions, for instance in mobilizing labor for agricultural projects and capital for emergency aid efforts for their members. Certainly the churches are becoming very important in these ways.

19. Of course, to call any kinship system "unilineal" or "bilateral" is to oversimplify. As Lewis has shown (1965), elements of a system such as descent reckoning and naming, residence, and the mobilization of groups for ritual or work may not follow the same principles. But the Luo demonstrate perhaps about as much consistency in patrilineal (and virilocal) principles as any known society in Africa or elsewhere (see Evans-Pritchard 1965; Shipton 1984b, 1985; Southall 1952). And by contrast, southwestern Colombian kinship systems, in the Andes and nearby lowlands, are clear cases of bilaterality in most respects, patronymy being one contrasting unilineal principle found there. Taussig noted (1980:85) that Cauca Valley had seen an increase in two-generational households headed by single women over the previous three decades, with a decrease in marriage rates.

20. In the Bolivian instance, "the mines eat us" refers to a fatal mining accident (Nash 1979:ix).

21. See Godoy 1985. He criticizes Taussig on other counts, including Taussig's rather simplistic portrait of "precapitalist" economies as closed, harmonious, supportive, redistributive systems. Taussig's neo-Marxist theoretical constructions are problematic in many ways, but they are interesting, and the ethnography valuable nonetheless.

22. Scott (1976:238–240), Fernandez (1978:214–215), and Ranger (1986) make similar points. Fernandez's concept, "argument of images," is a versatile one.

8

Conclusion

The Luo response to money, the market, and private property has been ambivalent and complex. The Luo have sold land and its most symbolically potent products for many decades, and they are doing so now on an unprecedented scale. But they are doing so with anxiety. The sales are sparking debate, challenging family unity, and further separating the real from the ideal in Luo behavior. For these rural Africans, in a sense, the real "black market" seems to be a white market. Regardless of one's theoretical or political persuasion, it is hard not to conclude that bitter money represents a reaction against new strains of possessive individualism in this rather egalitarian society, as devil's money represents in some Latin American contexts. The lineage-based conception of bitter money, however, is specifically African. The Luo emphasis on ancestors and bridewealth suggest that Luo have been trying to adjust to new experiences with older and more familiar local concepts. Bitter money contains a plea for personalized relations, and for the restitution of some family and community controls over vital resources. There is more to it than just an economic or political issue: there is also a motion for more autonomy in local culture. A sale of a bitter commodity is not a simple sale. It is a multifaceted transaction involving the autochthonous and the alien, the male and the female, the living and the dead.

Bitter money is a quintessentially anthropological phenomenon, in a traditional sense of the discipline: it is about economics, politics, law, kinship, the life cycle, and religion and ritual all at once. The anthropology to explain such a thing as this must be correspondingly multifaceted. It must not only consider symbolic polyvalence—the variety of things that the beliefs are consciously or unconsciously "about"—but it must also draw eclectically from diverse theoretical orientations in social science, accept multiple causes, and remain open to interpretations that seem on the surface to conflict.

To single out arbitrarily an economic dimension, liberalist "modernization" theories had a piece of the truth about the meaning of money in Luoland, in that no Luo today—even those who curse bitter money—will abjure shillings or the marketplace altogether. These things, foreign imports of the past century, are just too convenient, and in this respect they avowedly and undeniably represent to many Luo some kind of progress. Even multinational tobacco has an element of progress, as Luo elders will point out in surveying the hillsides of iron roofs (a way of trapping rain for clean water) it has bought for their neighborhoods. But Marxist-Leninism too offers a piece of the truth about cash and commodities: class splits seem to be widening today in rural Kenya,[1] as in rural Colombia, and these rifts are due in no small part to differential access to resources in new markets.[2] In simplistic, polarized debates between promarket "modernization" theories and Marxist theories, the truth is not just in the middle. It lies also in the extremities, and it may be in both at once. The Luo, like people everywhere, are quite capable of understanding money, or a commodity like tobacco, on more than one plane simultaneously.[3]

The heart of the lesson is pluralism. This is a lesson western Kenyans know well, as their deft handling of multiple languages suggests; and it is a lesson to which foreigners living among them might well pay more attention than they have.

The point applies equally to anthropology itself. If economic anthropology is to advance to maturity, it must at times regress to experimental play. It is wise neither to neglect one's forebears, nor to impose one of their directives in all contexts, but to break down, combine, and recombine their old lessons, like the shifting bits of glass in a kaleidoscope, in the light of the moment. The combinations are infinite. Recombining old notions eclectically may also yield some new truth, like a color wheel spun, revealing a hue not seen in any one of its sectors.

If anthropology is to issue any new concepts for discussion of African ambivalence about money, parts of them can be pieced together by *bricolage*, from the assorted pieces of theories now in discredit. As Stanley Barrett has shown,

> The image of anthropological theory as steady cumulation and progress is the ideal pattern; the actual pattern is quite different. The outstanding feature of anthropological theory has been its oscillating, pendulous nature, as it has swung back and forth between contradictory modes of explanation, sometimes reversing itself, sometimes repeating itself. . . . We keep discovering old truths, and long-abandoned orientations pop up again, often under new labels. [1984:74–76][4]

If we acknowledge that this is indeed one of the ways we advance, we may find new profit in currencies lately devalued: perhaps 1910s diffusionism, 1960s dependency theory, or even that fashion that seems destined so shortly for the scrap heap, 1980s deconstructionism. The theories to borrow and share are many. The trick, sometimes, is not to sell out to one.

Notes

1. See Hunt (1984), Kitching (1978), and Swainson (1980) on Kenya as a whole, and Goldenberg (1982) on the rural Luo, among many other available sources.

2. For a more modulated picture of agrarian class formation than Marx's or Lenin's, combining them with the theory of findings of A. V. Chayanov on family developmental cycles and on cyclical social mobility, see Shanin (1982).

3. Cf. Godelier's conclusions on salt trade among the Baruya of Papua New Guinea. He notes that the Baruya can consider salt as a gift in exchanges within a community, and as a commodity in exchanges outside (Godelier 1977:128). See also Gregory 1982:23.

4. Nor was this idea itself entirely new, as Barrett admits in citing Voget, Honigmann, Mirkovic, and Sahlins (S. Barrett 1984:74–76).

References Cited

Abe, Toshiharu
   1978   A Preliminary Report on Jachien among the Luo of South Nyanza.
   Institute of African Studies, University of Nairobi, discussion paper no.
   92.
Acland, J. D.
   1980[1971]   East African Crops. Hong Kong: Longman.
Akehurst, B. C.
   1981[1968]   Tobacco. London: Longman.
Antheaume, B.
   1974   Le Terroir d'Agbétiko. In Collection Atlas des Structures Agraires,
   no. 14. Paris: ORSTOM.
Appadurai, Arjun, ed.
   1986   The Social Life of Things: Commodities in Cultural Perspective. Cambridge: Cambridge University Press.
Aristotle
   1962[n.d.]   The Politics. T. A. Sinclair, trans. Harmondsworth: Penguin.
Barlett, Peggy, ed.
   1980   Agricultural Decision-Making: Anthropological Contributions to Development. New York: Academic Press.
Barra, G.
   1987[1939]   1,000 Kikuyu Proverbs. Nairobi: Kenya Literature Bureau.
Barrett, David B.
   1968   Schism and Renewal in Africa. Nairobi: Oxford University Press.
Barrett, David B., George K. Mambo, Janice McLaughlin, and Malcolm J.
McVeigh, eds.
   1973   Kenya Churches Handbook. Kisumu, Kenya: Evangel Publishing
   House.
Barrett, Stanley R.
   1984   The Rebirth of Anthropological Theory. Toronto: University of To-
   ronto Press.
Barth, Fredrik
   1967   Economic Spheres in Darfur. In Themes in Economic Anthropology.
   Raymond Firth, ed. Pp. 149–189. London: Tavistock.
Bates, Robert
   1983   Essays on the Political Economy of Africa. Cambridge: Cambridge
   University Press.
Beattie, John H. M.
   1966   Ritual and Social Change. Man (NS) 1:60–74.
   1971   The Nyoro State. Oxford: Oxford University Press.
Beckner, Morton
   1959   The Biological Way of Thought. New York: Columbia University
   Press.

Berry, Sara
1985   Fathers Work for their Sons. Berkeley: University of California Press.
Blount, Ben, and Louise Padgug-Blount
n.d.   Luo-English Dictionary. Institute of African Studies, University of Nairobi, Occasional Publication [unnumbered].
Bohannan, Paul
1955   Some Principles of Exchange and Investment among the Tiv. American Anthropologist 57:60–70.
1959   The Impact of Money on an African Subsistence Economy. Journal of Economic History 19(4):491–503. [Reprinted in Tribal and Peasant Economies. George Dalton, ed. New York: Natural History Press]
Bonacich, Edna, and John Modell
1980   The Economic Basis of Ethnic Solidarity. Berkeley: University of California Press.
Boomgard, James J., Stephen P. Davies, Steve Haggblade, and Donald C. Mead
1986   Subsector Analysis. East Lansing: Department of Agricultural Economics, Michigan State University, working paper 26.
Boswell, James
1917[1792]   Boswell's Life of Dr. Johnson. New York: Scribner's.
Bourdieu, Pierre
1977   Outline of a Theory of Practice. Cambridge: Cambridge University Press.
Brooks, Jerome E.
1937   Tobacco: Its History, Illustrated in the Books and Manuscripts of George Arents. New York: Rosenbach Company.
Bunker, Stephen G.
1986   Peasants and the State: The Economics of Market Control in Bugisu, Uganda, 1900–1983. Champaign: University of Illinois Press.
Busia, K. A.
1951   The Position of the Chief in the Modern Political System of Ashanti. London: Oxford University Press, for International African Institute.
Butterman, Judith
1979   Luo Social Formations in Change: Kanyamkago and Karachuonyo, c. 1800–1945. Ph.D. dissertation, Syracuse University.
Cardahi, C.
1955   Le Prêt à Intérêt et l'Usure. Revue Internationale de Droit Comparée 7:499–541.
Clastres, Pierre
1977   Society Against the State. New York: Urizen Books.
Coldham, Simon
1978   The Effect of Registration upon Customary Land Rights in Kenya. Journal of African Law 22(2):91–111.
1979   Land Tenure Reform in Kenya: The Limits of the Law. Journal of Modern African Studies 17(4):615–627.
Comaroff, Jean
1985   Body of Power, Spirit of Resistance: The Culture and History of a South African People. Chicago: University of Chicago Press.
Crazzolara, J. P.
1950   The Lwoo, Part I. Verona: Museum Combonianum.

Crump, Thomas
  1981   The Phenomenon of Money. London: Routledge & Kegan Paul.
DeWilde, John C.
  1967   Kenya: Central Nyanza District. In Experiences with Agricultural De-
    velopment in Tropical Africa, vol. II. John C. DeWilde, ed. Pp. 121–156.
    Baltimore: Johns Hopkins University Press.
Doig, Ivan
  1980   Winter Brothers. New York: Harcourt, Brace, Jovanovich.
Douglas, Mary
  1966   Purity and Danger. New York: Praeger.
Douglas, Mary, and Baron Isherwood
  1978   The World of Goods. Harmondsworth: Penguin.
Dundas, K. R.
  1913   The Wawanga and Other Tribes of the Elgon District, British East Af-
    rica. Journal of the Royal Anthropological Institute 43:19–75.
Durkheim, Emile
  1915[1912]   The Elementary Forms of the Religious Life. J. W. Swain, trans.
    London: Allen & Unwin.
Etzioni, Amitai, and Eva Etzioni-Harvey
  1964   Social Change. New York: Basic Books.
Evans-Pritchard, Edward E.
  1937   Witchcraft, Oracles and Magic among the Azande. London: Oxford
    University Press.
  1950   Ghostly Vengeance among the Luo of Kenya. Man 50(133):86–87.
  1956   Nuer Religion. London: Oxford University Press.
  1963   The Divine Kinship of the Shilluk of the Nilotic Sudan. In Essays in
    Social Anthropology. Edward Evans-Pritchard, ed. Pp. 66–86. New York:
    Free Press.
  1965[1949]   Luo Tribes and Clans. In The Position of Women in Society and
    Other Essays. E. Evans-Pritchard, ed. Pp. 228–244. London: Faber and
    Faber.
Fearn, Hugh
  1961   An African Economy: A Study of the Economic Development of the
    Nyanza Province of Kenya, 1903–1953. London: Oxford University Press.
Ferguson, James
  1985   The Bovine Mystique. Man (NS) 20:647–674.
Fernandez, James
  1978   African Religious Movements. Annual Review of Anthropology
    7:195–234.
Field, M. J.
  1940   The Social Organization of the Ga People. London: Crown Agents for
    the Colonies.
Firth, Raymond
  1967[1939]   Primitive Polynesian Economy. London: Routledge & Kegan
    Paul.
Fleuret, Ann, and Patrick Fleuret
  1980   Nutrition, Consumption and Agricultural Change. Human Organi-
    zation 39:250–260.
Foster, George
  1965   Peasant Society and the Image of the Limited Good. American An-
    thropologist 67:293–315.

Foster-Carter, Aidan
   1978   Can We Articulate "Articulation"? *In* The New Economic Anthropology. John Clammer, ed. Pp. 210–249. New York: St. Martin's Press.
Frobenius, Leo
   1898   Die Weltanschauung der Naturvölker. Weimar: E. Felber.
Geertz, Clifford
   1972   Deep Play: Notes on the Balinese Cockfight. Daedalus 101:1–37.
van Gennep, Arnold
   1960[1909]   The Rites of Passage. Monika B. Vizedom and Gabrielle A. Caffee, trans. Chicago: University of Chicago Press.
Glazier, Jack
   1985   Land and the Uses of Tradition among the Mbeere of Kenya. Lanham, Md.: University Press of America.
Godelier, Maurice
   1977   Perspectives in Marxist Anthropology. Cambridge: Cambridge University Press.
Godoy, Ricardo
   1985   Mining: Anthropological Perspectives. Annual Review of Anthropology 14:199–217.
Goldenberg, David A.
   1982   We Are All Brothers: The Suppression of Consciousness of Socio-Economic Differentiation in a Kenya Luo Lineage. Ph.D. dissertation, Brown University. Ann Arbor: University Microfilms International.
Goldsworthy, David
   1982   Tom Mboya: The Man Kenya Wanted to Forget. London: Heinemann.
Gregory, Christopher A.
   1982   Gifts and Commodities. New York: Academic Press.
Grindle, Merilee
   1986   State and Countryside. Baltimore: Johns Hopkins University Press.
Gudeman, Stephen
   1976   Relationships, Residence and the Individual: A Rural Panamanian Community. London: Routledge & Kegan Paul.
   1986   Economics as Culture: Models and Metaphors of Livelihood. London: Routledge & Kegan Paul.
Guyer, Jane
   1981   Household and Community in African Studies. African Studies Review 24(2–3):87–138.
Harris, Marvin
   1968   The Rise of Anthropological Theory. New York: Thomas Crowell.
Hart, Keith
   1982   The Political Economy of West African Agriculture. Cambridge: Cambridge University Press.
   1983   The Contribution of Marxism to Economic Anthropology. *In* Economic Anthropology: Topics and Theories. Sutti Ortiz, ed. Pp. 105–144. Lanham, Md.: University Press of America.
   1986   Heads or Tails: Two Sides of the Coin. Man 21(4):637–656.
Hauge, Hans-Egil
   1974   The Luo Religion and Folklore. Oslo: Universitets forlaget.
Haugerud, Angelique
   1983   The Consequences of Land Tenure Reform among Smallholders in the Kenyan Highlands. Rural Africana 15–16:65–89.

Hay, Margaret Jean
  1972 Economic Change in Luoland: Kowe, 1890–1945. Ph.D. dissertation.
        University of Wisconsin. Ann Arbor: University Microfilms International.
  1982 Women as Owners, Occupants, and Managers of Property in Colo-
        nial Western Kenya. *In* African Women and the Law: Historical Perspec-
        tives. Margaret Jean and Marcia Wright, eds. Pp. 110–123. Boston: Afri-
        can Studies Center, Boston University.
de Heusch, Luc
  1985 Sacrifice in Africa. Bloomington: Indiana University Press.
Hill, Polly
  1970 Studies in Rural Capitalism in West Africa. Cambridge: Cambridge
        University Press.
  1975 The West African Farming Household. *In* Changing Social Structure
        in Ghana. Jack Goody, ed. Pp. 119–136. London: International African In-
        stitute.
Hillman, James
  1982 A Contribution to *Soul and Money*. *In* Soul and Money. Russell A.
        Lockhart, James Hillman, Arwind Vasavada, John Weir Perry, Joel Co-
        vitz, and Adolf Guggenbuehl-Craig. Pp. 31–43. Dallas: Spring Publica-
        tions.
The Holy Bible
  King James Version. London: Oxford University Press.
Hubert, H., and M. Mauss
  1964[1898] Sacrifice: Its Nature and Function. W. D. Halls, trans. Chicago:
        University of Chicago Press.
Humphrey, Caroline
  1985 Barter and Economic Disintegration. Man (NS) 20(1):48–72.
Hunt, Diana
  1984 The Impending Crisis in Kenya: The Case for Land Reform. Brook-
        field, Vt.: Gower.
Iliffe, John
  1983 The Emergence of African Capitalism. Minneapolis: University of
        Minnesota Press.
Johnson, Steven Lee
  1980 Production, Exchange, and Economic Development among the Luo-
        Abasuba of Southwestern Kenya. Ph.D. dissertation, Indiana University.
        Ann Arbor: University Microfilms International.
Kenya Laws of Kenya. Nairobi: Government Printer.
Kenya Land Commission
  1934 Evidence and Memoranda. London: HMSO, United Kingdom Colo-
        nial Office (Col. 91).
Kenyatta, Jomo
  1965[1938] Facing Mount Kenya: The Tribal Life of the Gikuyu. London:
        Heinemann.
Kitching, Gavin
  1980 Class and Economic Change in Kenya. New Haven: Yale University
        Press.
Kuper, Adam
  1973 Anthropologists and Anthropology: The British School 1922–72. Har-
        mondsworth: Penguin.

Le Bris, E.
   1979   Suppression Démographique et Evolution Foncière; le Cas du Sud-
      est du Togo. *In* La Réforme Agro-Foncière dans les Pays du Conseil de
      l'Entente en Afrique de l'Ouest. African Perspectives (1). E. A. B. van
      Rouveroy van Nieuwaal and A. K. Amega, eds. Pp. 107–125. Leiden: Af-
      rika-Studiecentrum.
LeClair, Edward E., and Harold K. Schneider
   1968   Economic Anthropology. New York: Holt, Rinehart.
Lévi-Strauss, Claude
   1968   The Savage Mind. Chicago: University of Chicago Press.
Lewis, Ioan M.
   1965   Problems in the Comparative Study of Unilineal Descent. *In* The Rel-
      evance of Models for Social Anthropology. ASA Monographs I. Michael
      Banton, ed. Pp. 87–112. London: Tavistock.
Lienhardt, Godfrey
   1961   Divinity and Experience: The Religion of the Dinka. Oxford: Oxford
      University Press.
Litoux-Le Coq, M. C.
   1974   Fiata, Etude d'un Terroir dans le Sud-Togo-Lomé. Cyclostyled. Un-
      published MS.
Locke, John
   1960[1689]   Two Treatises of Government. Peter Laslett, ed. Cambridge:
      Cambridge University Press.
Lockhart, Russell A., James Hillman, Arwind Vasavada, John Weir Perry, Joel
Covitz, and Adolf Guggenbuehl-Craig
   1982   Soul and Money. Dallas: Spring Publications.
Long, Norman
   1968   Social Change and the Individual. Manchester: Manchester Univer-
      sity Press.
   1977   An Introduction to the Sociology of Rural Development. London:
      Tavistock.
Lonsdale, John
   1964   A Political History of Nyanza. Ph.D. dissertation, Cambridge Uni-
      versity.
Macfarlane, Alan
   1985   The Root of All Evil. *In* The Anthropology of Evil. David Parkin, ed.
      Pp. 57–76. Oxford: Blackwell.
MacPherson, C. B.
   1962   The Political Theory of Possessive Individualism. London: Oxford
      University Press.
Malcolm, David Wingfield
   1938   A Report on Land Utilization in Sukuma. Unpublished MS. Rhodes
      House Library, Oxford.
Malinowski, Bronislaw
   1922   Argonauts of the Western Pacific. London: Routledge.
   1935   Coral Gardens and their Magic. London: Allen & Unwin.
Marx, Karl
   1906[1867]   Capital: A Critique of Political Economy. Vol. I: The Process of
      Capitalist Production. Chicago: Charles H. Kerr and Co.
   1970[n.d.]   "Money." *In* Economics: Mainstream Readings and Radical
      Critiques. David Mermelstein, ed. Pp. 603–606. New York: Random
      House.

Mauss, Marcel
   1967[1925]   The Gift. Ian Cunnison, trans. New York: Norton.
Mboya, Paul
   1938   Luo—Kitgi gi Timbegi. Nairobi: East African Standard.
Mboya, Tom
   1970   The Challenge of Nationhood. New York: Praeger.
Meek, Charles Kingsley
   1946   Land Law and Custom in the Colonies. London: Oxford University
      Press.
Messer, Ellen
   1984   Anthropological Perspectives on Diet. Annual Review of Anthropol-
      ogy 13:205–249.
Moock, Joyce L.
   1986   Understanding Africa's Rural Households and Farming Systems.
      Boulder: Westview Press.
Moore, Sally Falk
   1986   Social Facts and Fabrications: "Customary" Law on Kilimanjaro,
      1880–1980. Cambridge: Cambridge University Press.
Murray, Colin
   1981   Families Divided: The Impact of Migrant Labour in Lesotho. Cam-
      bridge: Cambridge University Press.
Nash, June
   1979   We Eat the Mines. New York: Columbia University Press.
Neale, Walter C.
   1976   Monies in Societies. New York: Chandler and Sharp.
Needham, Rodney
   1975   Polythetic Classification. Man (NS) 10:349–367.
Northcote, G. A. S.
   1907   The Nilotic Kavirondo. Journal of the Royal Anthropological Institute
      38:58–66.
Ocholla-Ayayo, A. B. C.
   1976   Traditional Ideology and Ethics among the Southern Luo. Uppsala:
      Scandinavian Institute of African Studies.
   1979   Marriage and Cattle Exchange among the Nilotic Luo. Paideuma
      25:173–193.
   1980   The Luo Culture. Wiesbaden: Franz Steiner Verlag.
Odinga, Oginga
   1967   Not Yet Uhuru. London: Heinemann.
Ogot, Bethwell A.
   1967   Peoples of East Africa: History of the Southern Luo. Vol. I: Migration
      and Settlement 1500–1900. Nairobi: East African Publishing House.
Okoth-Ogendo, H. W. O.
   1976   African Land Tenure Reform. In Agricultural Development in Kenya.
      Judith Heyer, J. K. Maitha, and W. M. Senga, eds. Pp. 152–185. Nairobi:
      Oxford University Press.
   1978   The Political Economy of Land Law: An Essay in the Legal Organi-
      zation of Underdevelopment in Kenya, 1895–1974. D.S.L. thesis, Yale
      University.
Ortiz, Sutti
   1983   What Is Decision Analysis About? In Economic Anthropology. Sutti
      Ortiz, ed. Pp. 249–300. Lanham, Md.: University Press of America.

Ortner, Sherry
   1984   Anthropological Theory since the Sixties. Comparative Studies in Society and History 26(1):126–166.
Ousmane, Sembene [né Ousmane Sembene]
   1985[1960]   God's Bits of Wood. London: Heinemann.
Pala, Achola Okeyo
   1977   Changes in Economy and Ideology: A Study of the Juluo of Kenya
   (with Special Reference to Women). Ph.D. dissertation, Harvard University.
   1980   Daughters of the Lakes and Rivers: Colonization and the Land Rights
   of Luo Women in Kenya. *In* Women and Colonization: Anthropological
   Perspectives. Mona Etienne and Eleanor Leacock, eds. Pp. 186–213. New
   York: Praeger.
   1983   Women's Access to Land and Their Role in Agriculture and Decision-
   Making on the Farm: Experiences of the Joluo of Kenya. Journal of Eastern
   African Research and Development 13:69–87.
Parsons, Elsie Clews
   1936   Mitla: Town of the Souls. Chicago: University of Chicago Press.
Parkin, David J.
   1972   Palms, Wine and Witnesses. San Francisco: Chandler.
   1978   The Cultural Definition of Political Response: Lineal Destiny among
   the Luo. New York: Academic Press.
   1980   Kind Bridewealth and Hard Cash. *In* The Meaning of Marriage Payments. John Comaroff, ed. Pp. 197–220. New York: Academic Press.
Parkin, David J., ed.
   1985   The Anthropology of Evil. Oxford: Blackwell.
Polanyi, Karl
   1944   The Great Transformation: The Political and Economic Origins of Our
   Time. Boston: Beacon Press.
The Qur'an
   Published as The Meaning of the Glorious Qur'an (1971), Marmaduke Pick-
   thall, trans. Beirut: Dar al-Kitab Allubnani Publishers.
Ranger, Terence O.
   1986   Religious Movements and Politics in Sub-Saharan Africa. African
   Studies Review 29(2):1–70.
Richards, Audrey I.
   1939   Land, Labour and Diet in Northern Rhodesia. London: Oxford University Press.
   1940   The Bemba Tribe of North-Eastern Rhodesia. *In* African Political Systems. Meyer Fortes and Edward Evans-Pritchard, eds. Pp. 83–120. London: Oxford University Press, for International African Institute.
Robertson, A. F.
   1984   People and the State: An Anthropology of Planned Development.
   Cambridge: Cambridge University Press.
   1987   The Dynamics of Productive Relationships: African Share Contracts
   in Comparative Perspective. Cambridge: Cambridge University Press.
Rodinson, Maxime
   1974[1966]   Islam and Capitalism. Brian Pearce, trans. London: Allen Lane,
   Division of Penguin Books.
Sahlins, Marshall
   1972   Stone Age Economics. Chicago: Aldine.

Saul, John, and G. Arrighi
1973 Essays on the Political Economy of Africa. New York: Monthly Review Press.
Schacht, Joseph
1984[1964] An Introduction to Islamic Law. Oxford: Clarendon Press.
Schneider, Harold K.
1974 Economic Man: The Anthropology of Economics. New York: Free Press.
Schweinfurth, George
1878[1873] The Heart of Africa. Vol. I. London: Sampson, Low.
Scott, James
1976 The Moral Economy of the Peasant. New Haven: Yale University Press.
Shakespeare, William
1969[c.1608–9] The Life of Timon of Athens. *In* William Shakespeare: Complete Works. Baltimore: Penguin.
Shanin, Teodor
1982 Polarization and Cyclical Mobility: The Russian Debate over the Differentiation of the Peasantry. *In* Rural Development: Theories of Peasant Economy and Agrarian Change. John Harriss, ed. Pp. 223–245. London: Hutchinson.
Shanklin, Eugenia
1985 Sustenance and Symbol: Anthropological Studies of Domesticated Animals. Annual Review of Anthropology 14:375–403.
Shipton, Parker
1984a Lineage and Locality as Antithetical Principles in East African Systems of Land Tenure. Ethnology 23(2):117–132.
1984b Strips and Patches: A Demographic Dimension in Some African Landholding and Political Systems. Man (NS) 19:613–634.
1985 Land, Credit, and Crop Transitions in Kenya: The Luo Response to Directed Development in Nyanza Province. Ph.D. dissertation, Cambridge University. Ann Arbor: University Microfilms International.
1988 The Kenyan Land Tenure Reform: Misunderstandings in the Public Creation of Private Property. *In* Land and Society in Contemporary Africa. Richard E. Downs and Stephen P. Reyna, eds. Pp. 91–135. Hanover, N.H.: University Press of New England.
Simmel, Georg
1978[1907] The Philosophy of Money. Tom Bottomore and David Frisby, trans. Boston: Routledge & Kegan Paul.
Smith, G. Elliot
1928 In the Beginning: The Origin of Civilization. New York: Morrow.
Southall, Aidan
1952 Lineage Formation among the Luo. International African Institute Memorandum 26. Pp. 1–43. London: Oxford University Press.
Stafford, R. L.
1967 An Elementary Luo Grammar with Vocabularies. Nairobi: Oxford University Press.
Stichter, Sharon
1982 Migrant Labour in Kenya: Capitalism and African Response. London: Longman.

Swainson, Nicola
1980 The Development of Corporate Capitalism in Kenya, 1918–1977. London: Heinemann.
Taussig, Michael
1980 The Devil and Commodity Fetishism in South America. Chapel Hill: University of North Carolina Press.
Temu, A.
1972 British Protestant Missions in Kenya: 1873–1929. London: Longmans.
Turner, Victor
1969 The Ritual Process: Structure and Anti-Structure. Chicago: Aldine.
Wagner, Gunter
1949 (vol. I) 1956 (vol. II) The Bantu of North Kavirondo. London: Oxford University Press.
Waligorski, Andrzej
1970 Les Marchés des Luo vers 1946–1948. Africana Bulletin (Warsaw) 11:9–24.
Weber, Max
1947[1904] The Theory of Social and Economic Organization. A. M. Henderson and Talcott Parsons, trans. New York: Oxford University Press.
1958[1904] The Protestant Ethic and the Spirit of Capitalism. Talcott Parsons, trans. New York: Scribner's.
Whisson, Michael G.
1962a The Will of God and the Wiles of Men: An Examination of the Beliefs Concerning the Supernatural Held by the Luo with Particular Reference to Their Functions in the Field of Social Control. East African Institute of Social Research Conference Papers, Makerere University College, Kampala.
1962b The Journeys of the JoRamogi. East African Institute of Social Research Conference Papers, Makerere University College, Kampala.
1964 Change and Challenge: A Study of the Social and Economic Changes among the Kenya Luo. Nairobi: Christian Council of Kenya.
Whitehead, Ann
1981 I'm Hungry, Mum: The Politics of Domestic Budgeting. *In* Of Marriage and the Market: Women's Subordination in International Perspective. Kate Young, Carol Wolkowitz, and Roslyn McCullagh, eds. Pp. 88–111. London: CSE Books.
Wilks, Ivor
1967 Ashanti Government. *In* West African Kingdoms in the Nineteenth-Century. Daryll Forde and Phyllis Kaberry, eds. Pp. 206–238. London: Oxford University Press, for International African Institute.
Willis, Roy
1973 An Indigenous Critique of Colonialism: The Fipa of Tanzania. *In* Anthropology and the Colonial Encounter. Talal Asad, ed. Pp. 246–256. London: Ithaca Press.
Wilson, Gordon
1961 Luo Customary Laws and Marriage Laws Customs [sic]. Nairobi: Government Printer.
1967[1960] Homicide and Suicide among the Joluo of Kenya. *In* African Homicide and Suicide. Paul Bohannan, ed. Pp. 179–213. New York: Atheneum.

Wipper, Audrey
  1977   Rural Rebels: A Study of Two Protest Movements in Kenya. London:
    Oxford University Press.
Wittgenstein, Ludwig
  1958   Preliminary Studies for the "Philosophical Investigations," Generally
    Known as The Blue and Brown Books. Oxford: Blackwell.
Yusuf, Ahmed Beita
  1975   Capital Formation and Management among the Muslim Hausa Trad-
    ers of Kano, Nigeria. Africa 45(2):167–182.